Mastering Approaches to Diversity in Social Work

Mastering Social Work Skills series

Edited by Jane Wonnacott

This series of short, accessible books focuses on the everyday key skills that social workers need in order to practise effectively and ensure the best possible outcomes for service users. Easy to read and practical, the books feature key learning points, practice examples based on real-life situations, and exercises for the reader to enhance their learning. The books in this series are essential reading for post-qualifying social work students and social work practitioners.

Jane Wonnacott is Director of In-Trac Training and Consultancy, UK.

other books in the series

Mastering Social Work Supervision

Jane Wonnacott

ISBN 978 1 84905 774 1

MASTERING

Approaches to Diversity in Social Work

Linda Gast and Anne Patmore

Jessica Kingsley *Publishers*
London and Philadelphia

Figure 2.1 has been reproduced with the consent of Conroy Grizzle.
Tables 3.1, 3.2, 3.3 and 3.4 reproduced with permission from Hofstede.
Figure 4.3 from Morrison 2001.

First published in 2012
by Jessica Kingsley Publishers
116 Pentonville Road
London N1 9JB, UK
and
400 Market Street, Suite 400
Philadelphia, PA 19106, USA

www.jkp.com

Library of Congress Cataloging in Publication Data
Gast, Linda Eileen, 1954-
  Mastering approaches to diversity in social work / Linda Gast and Anne
Patmore ; foreword by Jane Wonnacott.
      p. cm. -- (Mastering social work skills)
  Includes bibliographical references and index.
  ISBN 978-1-84905-224-5 (alk. paper)
  1. Social service. 2. Diversity in the workplace. 3. Social service and
race relations. I. Patmore, Anne, 1953- II. Title.
  HV40.G38 2012
  361.3068'3--dc23
                          2011032356

British Library Cataloguing in Publication Data
A CIP catalogue record for this book is available from the British Library

ISBN 978 1 84905 224 5
eISBN 978 0 85700 458 1

Printed and bound in Great Britain

Contents

Figures and Tables

Series Editor Foreword

Working effectively with diversity is at the heart of all social work practice. However, too often social workers hear the phrase and become de-skilled fearful of making mistakes and concerned that they may be failing to adequately address all aspects of a person's identity. This book recognises the complexity of the task but aims to make working with diversity 'ordinary' and equip social workers with a number of useful tools to help them work together with service users to provide help to meet need across all dimensions of the service user's life. Along with all other books in this series, it is a practical text using material that has been delivered to many social workers attending training courses over a number of years. It challenges readers to think broadly about the topic, consider their own practice and develop new ways of thinking and working.

PREFACE

If you talk to a man in a language he understands, that goes to his head.

If you talk to him in his language that goes to his heart.

Nelson Mandela

This book is about the complexity of the world in which social workers operate. It explores some of the dimensions of 'otherness'; how people can be so different to ourselves that we find it difficult to understand the rationale for their behaviours. Having models to make sense of these differences means that they become understandable and cannot be attributed to 'personality conflicts' or because 'they' come from a different culture. Although aimed at practitioners, supervisors, practice teachers and assessors will also find this book helpful by using the models to explore interactions between workers and service users, and to encourage practitioners to reflect on how their culture impacts on others. Good practice that pays attention to diversity is good practice per se, as most service users wish to be identified as unique human beings and worked with according to their own individual experiences.

The book could not have been written without the encouragement of many colleagues, including the late Dr Tony Morrison for his inspirational leadership, colleagues at In-Trac for their critically supportive commentaries and Alison Bishop for her technical wizardry, Phil Taylor for the introduction of the Jungian approach and Myers–Briggs Type Indicators into mainstream social work practice, and Conroy Grizzle, for the development of his model for understanding racism. We also wish to thank the many practitioners who have been trained using these models and have contributed to their development and refinement, and the students and practitioners we have worked with over the years who have informed our thinking. Lastly, our thanks to Mike and Peter, our respective partners, without whose unfailing support this book would not have been possible.

CHAPTER 1

Diversity in the Context of Current Social Work Practice

Key messages

- Diversity is a broad subject, related to equal opportunities, anti-oppressive practice and anti-discriminatory practice.

- Social workers need to understand their own prejudices, biases, stereotypes and opinions and how these may impact on practice.

- In order to work effectively with the diverse range of service users, any discrimination and oppression which they may have experienced needs to be acknowledged.

- Power impacts on how people experience the world, so is a crucial component of any social work relationship.

Introduction

Diversity is an important yet difficult area to talk and write about. It raises strong emotions in many people precisely because it touches on all of our lives and has personal resonances. Whatever we write as authors has the potential to be biased because of our genders, our racial backgrounds, our age, our abilities, our education and our perspectives. However, as well as the more obvious areas in which people have experienced discrimination, we have chosen to cover some broader differences, to extend thinking about difference. When the National Minimum Standards for Adoption (DfE 2011) were published, Standard 2, expressed as 'Promoting a positive identity, potential and valuing diversity', elicited anxiety that this would dilute the focus on areas traditionally associated with oppression or discrimination, yet it seems to offer a much more holistic and comprehensive appreciation of the complexity of individuals.

This book seeks to explore racial, cultural and personal diversity from a number of different perspectives using a range of models, some of which are very familiar to the social care professions but some of which are not. It will explore personal biases which affect the way in which we perceive others and some of the values by which we make judgements about individual, family, group and community differences. It will then offer models for understanding diversity which, with practice, can positively influence the quality of interactions with service users. We intend for this book to be an opportunity to explore the big picture of diversity and to provide the reader with the knowledge and awareness needed to practice social work responsibly and effectively. Working from the starting point that diversity is 'all the ways in which we differ' (the approach taken by the authors) and 'everybody is like all other people, like some other people, and like no other person' (a concept explored by Kluckhohn and Murray 1948), diversity focuses particularly on the middle phrase – how we are like others and how we differ.

Points to consider

- What does diversity mean to you?
- What areas of diversity are particularly important to you and why?
- How would you explain these to others?
- What are the areas of diversity that you haven't paid as much attention to yet?
- How will you use this book to help you develop your knowledge and confidence in these areas?

This should have started you thinking about the ways in which you are different from every other person, but also how you are linked with others. Society tends to assess individual uniqueness against human universality, and one key area of difference which is very important is cultural specificity. Those who live in a white euro-centric society (i.e. a society which sees the rest of the world from the perspective of its own values and ways of doing things) can devalue colleagues and service users from other cultures. This means that a practitioner has the ability to impose their own values and outlook on their work and fail to take into account cultural differences, if not being careful and alert to the potential for this. At the same time services users can impose their values too ('it is like this in our culture') if the worker is not knowledgeable and confident enough to challenge this. Experience has shown that if these attitudes are not challenged it can lead to dangerous practice. To address this we will be describing several tools which allow us to assess individuals for their similarity to, and differences from, other people, to build up a unique picture of the person with whom we are working; but it is important to remember how much we are influenced by the society in which we grow up, and how we unthinkingly absorb the influences of that society.

Historically, the approaches which organisations have taken have included promoting anti-discriminatory practice, anti-oppressive practice and equal opportunities, but the difference between them has frequently been vague and the terms used interchangeably, in an unhelpful way. Diversity is one of the areas of language and behaviour where there can be a great deal of confusion and anxiety about what is expected, what is appropriate and how easy it can be to get things wrong. In the past in local authorities there has been an emphasis on not using language which could be seen as in any way offensive, for example 'black coffee and white coffee', a feeling about 'political correctness' and not daring to say anything for fear of getting it wrong. In order to be a positive organisation, which is able to work with vulnerable people, we believe that this anxiety is unhelpful, and leads to guarded and restricted communication. What is needed is for us to be sensitive to other people's differences, and hold to an intention to avoid knowingly saying or doing anything which is inappropriate. Within this we will get things wrong, but if we are prepared to explain to others about our sensitivities, apologise if we do get it wrong and learn from the experience to do things differently, then it is not so difficult. What we are talking about is respecting each other, showing consideration for difference, and spending time getting to know each other. It's not rocket science! What we have tried to do in this book is introduce some knowledge, information and thoughts about how we can best work with other people, acknowledging and valuing difference.

Early equal opportunities or anti-racism training was often experienced as confrontational, and made some white, middle-class, non-disabled men feel as though they were 'the problem', and that they were the oppressors as they were seen to be the group with the most power.

Since then organisations have moved on to providing diversity training of a more positive style, but this is often still approached with suspicion. Staff in some organisations have seen diversity training as just the 'up-to-date' version of equality training or as jumping on a politically correct bandwagon.

Understanding the concept of diversity and its relevance to social work

Recognising and respecting diversity and individuality is the cornerstone of social work practice. The International Federation of Social Workers website (2004), in their Ethics in Social Work, Statement of Principles state: 'Recognising diversity – Social workers should recognise and respect the ethnic and cultural diversity of the societies in which they practice, taking account of individual, family, group and community differences.'

The General Social Care Council (GSCC) *Code of Practice for Social Care Workers* (2010) includes within code 1:

1.1 treating each person as an individual

1.5 promoting equal opportunities for service users and carers

1.6 respecting diversity and different cultures and values.

These are values which most social workers are very happy to espouse, but can prove more difficult to uphold in the pressures of day-to-day practice. It is important to have a range of conceptual frameworks around diversity to inform all engagements with service users.

Exploring the range of diversity

The list of differences which apply to people is almost endless, but it is useful to categorise some of these, so that we can be clear what we are talking about (Table 1.1). Many of these characteristics could be in more than one column, but we have tried to not repeat things too often.

Table 1.1 Exploring the range of diversity

Primary characteristics	Secondary characteristics
These are features that are immediately visible when we first see someone: Male/female. Approximate age. Skin colour. Height. Weight – relating to size. Visible disabilities. Style of dress. Body markings (tattoos, etc.). Decoration (jewellery, etc.).	These are features which require us to start to get to know the person and are not immediately obvious: Non-visible disabilities (hearing impairment, learning disability etc). Language. Accent. Personal preferences (see Chapter 5). Personal history and upbringing.
Workplace characteristics	Characteristics we might use in work with service users
These are features which impact on us in the workplace: Full/part time. Hierarchical status. Homecare responsibilities. Learning styles. Motivation about work.	These are features which we might well be required to take into account when working with service users: Style of parenting/caregiving. Levels of personal hygiene. Diet. Cleanliness of the home. Gender differentiation of roles.

All of these characteristics affect how we initially respond to others as we notice and learn about each individual's characteristics; we can modify our responses as we get to know people.

Points to consider

- What other characteristics could you add to each of these boxes?

- Which characteristics in someone might have a particular impact on you?

- What might you need to do to become more alert to your perceptions of these characteristics?

It is important to explore the similarities and differences between equal opportunities and diversity.

Equal opportunities

Equal opportunities addresses the areas of difference covered by legislation, which is more limited than the broad span of diversity. The Equality Act 2010 replaced previous anti-discrimination legislation and introduced new protections and concepts which will require some re-thinking from what has become accepted practice.

The Equality Act 2010 covers nine protected characteristics, which cannot be used as a reason to treat people unfairly. Every person has one or more of the protected characteristics, so the act protects everyone against unfair treatment.

The protected characteristics are

- Sex.
- Race, which legally covers nationality, ethnicity, colour and culture.
- Disability.
- Religion or belief.
- Age.
- Sexual orientation.
- Gender reassignment.
- Marriage and civil partnership.
- Pregnancy and maternity.

Equal opportunities are externally driven, for if organisations are not adhering to equal opportunities requirements there can be external repercussions, and legal action can follow. An organisation can decide to cover more than the current protected characteristics, but they cannot do less. Even so, equality of opportunity has some clear statements of intent linked closely to diversity:

> Ensuring equality of opportunity does not mean that all children are treated the same. It does mean understanding and working sensitively and knowledgeably with diversity to identify the particular issues for a child and his/her family, taking account of experiences and family context. (Department of Health, Department for Education and Employment, and Home Office 2000 para 1.43, p.12)

Diversity

Diversity has been driven by the internal agendas of organisations, springing from the business case for achieving the best possible workforce and getting the best out of staff. There is no legislation about diversity, so there will be no external repercussions if it is not valued, but organisations taking this approach are driven by quality and focus on potential. It is often about an organisation wanting to become an employer of choice and staff choosing it because it offers consideration, flexibility according to need, and appreciation of what each person can contribute.

Table 1.2 Comparison between equal opportunities and diversity

Equal opportunities	Diversity
Based on the limited number of areas covered by legislation.	Covering all areas of difference.
Externally initiated – is imposed on an organisation whether it is wanted or not.	Internally initiated – only happens in organisations if they are interested.
Legally driven – if there is non-compliance there are legal consequences.	Business needs driven – there are no legal consequences, only the desire to be an employer of choice.
Quantitative focus – meeting targets or quotas.	Qualitative focus – seeking the best possible staff.
Problem focused – to avoid threats of legal action.	Opportunity focused – to bring out the best in all staff.
Reactive – follows on from the legislation, doing what is necessary and setting the necessary policy framework.	Proactive – positively promoting and valuing all contributions and seeking to expand the diversity of the workforce.
Covers the protected characteristics.	All differences.

The National Occupational Standards for Social Work (TOPSS 2002) make it clear that social workers should have a good knowledge of the relevant legislation and challenge discriminatory practices. Social work values also require a commitment to respect difference and an ability to respond appropriately to all diversity issues.

Points to consider

- How does the legislation impact on your particular area of work?

- What are the areas of diversity you may need to pay particular attention to in your area of work?

The legislation is the foundation for social work, however, as Thompson (2011) says: 'A narrow, legalistic approach is unlikely to challenge discrimination effectively and does not therefore merit the title – "anti-discriminatory"' (p.90). To move from the legislation into practice requires an examination of this concept and that of anti-oppressive practice.

Anti-discriminatory practice

This concept comes from the notion of equal opportunities and recognises that certain groups do not have equality of opportunity because of discrimination at both a personal and institutional level. The Equality Act 2010 is dealt with in more detail in Chapter 2, but the principles underpinning anti-discriminatory practice have been important in the development of social work values. It stems from awareness that some people do not enjoy the same access to services as others, and that services provided often reflect the dominant cultural norms of the organisation or of society. One example where this is clearly expressed in terms of race is in the definition of institutional racism in the McPherson Enquiry into the death of Stephen Lawrence as:

> The collective failure of an organisation to provide an appropriate and professional service to people because of their colour, culture or ethnic origin. It can be seen or detected in the processes, attitudes and behaviour which amount to discrimination through unwitting prejudice, ignorance, thoughtlessness and racist stereotyping which disadvantage minority ethnic people. (McPherson 2001, para 6.34, p.28)

The aims of anti-discriminatory practice therefore are:

- to offer a service that does not restrict access to any particular group

- to challenge perceived forms of discrimination in service provision

- to offer culturally sensitive services and practices to all.

Anti-oppressive practice

Thompson (2011) states that 'one of the main outcomes of discrimination is oppression' (p.90). Anti-oppressive practice derives from an analysis of power and inequality in society and how dominant groups use power to oppress others and thus preserve their own position. Institutions in society whether they are family structures, welfare agencies or political and legal systems, are used to maintain the current power positions and can therefore help to perpetuate oppression.

In social work terms, people are aware that social control measures are used disproportionately in respect of certain groups who are seen as 'problematic' and in need of control, such as the overuse of stop and search legislation with young African-Caribbean and Asian men. There will also be an awareness that policy and practice can exploit people or re-enforce inequality.

The aim of anti-oppressive practice therefore gives rise to a practice position which:

- tries not to abuse its power

- works to counteract abuse of power elsewhere

- works to empower all service users, to assist in the process of people taking control of their own lives.

Power – its use in social work

Power is inherent in the role of a social worker. Social workers are commonly seen as the 'gatekeepers' to services, with the power to provide or withhold increasingly scarce resources. The ability to recommend that a child be taken away from its parents, a mentally ill person be committed to a hospital or a young offender receive a custodial sentence offers the practitioner a very powerful position in relation to service users. In recognition of this there are several models for exploring the power relationship. One of the most frequently used and helpful is Thompson's (2011) 'PCS analysis', which explores the way in which inequalities of power and opportunity operate at three separate and inter-related levels – personal, cultural and structural. The personal considers how thoughts, feelings and actions at an individual level can have a significant bearing on inequality and oppression; the cultural relates to commonalities, consensus and conformity across groups; while the structural comprises the macro-level influences and constraints of the various social, political and economic aspects of the contemporary social order.

French and Raven (1959) identify different sources of power, all of which are relevant to the practice of social work and impact on the relationship between social worker and service user.

1. Legitimate (or positional) power

This is the formal authority given by the position of practitioner in an organisational hierarchy, exercised in relation to service users and by managers in relation to staff. A role gives the occupier the right to exercise authority as defined by the boundaries of that role. It is seen in the job title, uniform, badge of office and form of address. Legitimate power creates an obligation to accept it and be influenced by it.

Legitimate power comes from three main sources:

- The prevailing values of society, organisations or group determine what is legitimate and what values will be internalised by the individual, for example, some societies give legitimate power to older people.

- People can obtain legitimate power from the accepted social structure, for example, accepted ruling class.

- From being the designated agent or representative of a powerful person or a group, for example, elected officials.

In social work terms the legitimate power is given by legislation to individuals to exercise controlling behaviours on behalf of society. The extent of these powers, or the frequency or ease with which they are used, is frequently misrepresented by the media and misunderstood by many people in the general population, such as the perceived practice of taking children into care at the slightest provocation.

2. Reward power

Reward power represents the carrot in a 'carrot and stick' situation. It is the extent to which an individual has the capacity to reward another for compliance and the extent to which this is recognised by both parties.

The rewards are not just financial but also giving assistance, lending resources, being cooperative, sharing information, advancement, recognition, networks, contacts, personal support, favourable work, more responsibility, and new technology. Service users must value the rewards for this to be effective, and must also believe that the practitioner has the power, for example, to influence those higher up in the matter of allocation of resources, or for staff to believe managers can influence promotions. Power-seekers look to accumulate and control desired organisational resources in order to be able to use them in exchange for compliance and reciprocal favours.

3. Coercive power

This is the stick in a 'carrot and stick' situation. If the person with the power has the capacity to operate sanctions or punishments against an employee, service user or any 'other', for behaviour unwanted by the person with power, then they have a coercive base of power.

It is the ability to punish or to threaten to punish and is based on fear. It results in unwilling compliance, which is harmful to the organisation in the long term as it damages trust and willingness to cooperate, and produces an atmosphere of distrust and fear. It is damaging with service users as it means they are much more likely to be manipulative and try to hide any behaviours that might be thought to encourage the use of coercive power. Managers wield coercive power through disciplinary procedures, ultimate dismissal, and payment systems. Practitioners use power through differential use of resources, or more punitive approaches to particular groups. It is the fear of punishment for not following the rules of the organisations, such as getting to work on time or looking busy when the boss appears, which produces apparently good behaviour. Compliance may be an immediate response, but longer term commitment is unlikely.

4. Expert power

If a worker or service user perceives another as having key knowledge or a specialised skill that they themselves do not possess, then the latter has a potent source of power over the former. This increases when decisions made by the expert are shown to be right. It is recognisable in the extent to which others attribute knowledge and expertise.

To accumulate expert power people need to foster an image of experience and competence and avoid making rash decisions, to preserve mystique and never make anything look easy. There is also the need to be perceived as credible and trustworthy. Credibility may come from having the right credentials, and tangible evidence of these may be seen in certificates and diplomas displayed in offices. Another example of a way of establishing expert power is when a social worker gives their qualifications and details of their experience and expertise in a court setting.

5. Referent power

This source of power is derived from personal qualities and attraction. Of all the bases of power this is the only one not related to position within the organisation. One person perceives the other to have power because they are attractive, have desirable resources or personal characteristics. This is sometimes referred to as 'charismatic authority'. This can be very productive, but may also be dangerous if the source of power does not use it with integrity.

6. Information power

This is an additional source, added by Buchanan and Huczynski (1991). 'Information is power' and is the lifeblood of organisations. It is similar to expert power but the person to whom the power is given is not the expert on the subject, but the one with information not possessed by others. People using informational power need to be positioned in networks through which relevant information flows, such as trades unions or the particular part of an organisation where information is received or processed. The person needs to be involved in the internal and external communication flow of the organisation.

The power structure within an organisation is not necessarily linked to the formal organisational structure and to seniority. The bases of power overlap, and any one individual may draw on several.

Implications for social work and diversity

Whenever a social worker meets a service user there is an immediate power relationship, and yet many people coming into social work are uncomfortable with the power invested in them in their role. This can be demonstrated by trying to minimise the inherent power ('I am only here to try to help you,' rather than, 'I am here to assess whether I might need to do something about your situation,'). Alternatively, it may be a rather aggressive use of power, possibly because the worker is using a preference from their shadow side (see Chapter 5), and where, because they are not confident about this, they use it in an awkward and clumsy way.

Empowerment

Empowerment has become an increasingly significant concept in social work over the last two decades, although different people mean different things by it, and many consider it to be a term that is often invoked without really being understood or explained. The International Federation of Social Workers definition of social work includes reference to 'the empowerment and liberation of people to enhance well-being' (IFSW 2000), and their principles include social workers' responsibility to respect the right to self-determination and promote the right to participation of people using services 'in ways that enable them to be empowered in all aspects of decisions and actions affecting their lives' (IFSW 2004). The UK National Occupations Standards for Social Work (TOPSS 2002) also makes it clear that empowering individuals, families, carers, groups and communities to represent their views and have them considered in decisions affecting them underpins all social work practice. In practice empowerment is about the service user having choice and control in their own life, and being seen as the expert about their life and what they want to achieve. Whilst few would dispute this as being fair and desirable, many service users and groups would argue that it is not their experience.

Points to consider

I have attended meetings about my son and daughter. There were lots of people there, not sure what it was called, but it was the most intimidating place I have ever been to. They just talked about me (para 3.6, p.14).

Many people suffer from nerves. That (the case conference) would push you over the edge. I felt stuck, unable to speak, unable to think at all. It was like being in a dream where it is all going on, but there is nothing you can do about it (para 3.6, p.15).

The person I met before the conference was very nice and kind, but I did not really understand what she said.

You cannot complain, if you do you will get into more trouble with them (the social workers) and so it's best to say nothing. Anyway no one will listen to you, as you are not a professional (para 3.7, p.16).

If they are rude and disrespectful and you feel judged, you're not going to invite them in. People need to feel supported and listened to (para 4.4, p.19).

I went to another meeting after the case conferences, and that was OK. There were less people there and we talked about what would help me and my six kids. I thought finally someone understands me. Something good came out of it for us. We got help. I could go through all of it, if I knew it would end in help (para 3.6, p.16).

Trust is important to make a partnership. To understand each other's needs and work together (para 4.3, p.19).

(Wiffin 2010)

- What do these quotes from service users tell you about their experience of having choice and control when in the child protection system?
- What was disempowering?
- What was empowering?

People who have come to believe they are worthless, stupid, or unimportant, those with a negative story of the world (see p.25), are likely to find it difficult to see themselves as having expertise, even in their own lives, or to have the confidence and courage to move forward, explore new areas and take risks. Many of the people social workers support have had their confidence undermined so often, and have experienced discrimination and oppression so frequently, that enabling them to empower themselves is likely to take time and commitment.

Points to consider

She started off by saying, 'I am going to be honest with you,' and this led to a ten minute look at what was wrong with our family. I was tempted to say, 'I am going to be honest with you,' but you cannot do it, can you? So we all sat there and listened to how bad we were as a family. And secretly, as this was my only power, I thought I am not going to tell you anything. (Wiffin 2010, p.32)

- How would you know if this was what was happening to you?

- How could you work against this happening?

- What might it be about you and your approach which a service user could find intimidating, so lead them to behave like this with you?

- How do you ensure that you are working to empower your service users?

In adult services, empowerment has taken a prominent place in the consideration of access to services and choices about delivery methods, even if it means allowing service users to make decisions that the service providers disagree with (DoH 2010).

> Personalised care is for everyone, but some people will need more support than others to make choices about how they live their lives. Everyone has the right to personalised care and as much choice and control as possible. As we pick up the pace on personalisation, we need to ensure that this includes the most vulnerable members of our society, including those who may lack capacity. With effective personalisation comes the need to manage risk for people to make decisions as safely as possible. Making risks clear and understood is crucial to empowering service users and carers, recognising people as 'experts in their own lives'. (DoH 2010, Sect. 6.9)

Story of the world

Our 'story of the world' is a more friendly term for cognitive schemata as described by McGuire (2000). It is the set of beliefs, developed from our upbringing, culture, society and perspectives, which affects our approach to everything we see and then how we interpret and respond. Understanding this as each person's starting point for their interactions with the world forms the basis of the cognitive behavioural approach to work with individuals.

Table 1.3 Exercise

Think of a time and situation when you have had the feelings in each of these boxes:

Powerful and comfortable	Powerful and uncomfortable
Powerless and comfortable	Powerless and uncomfortable

- What made the comfortable ones acceptable?
- What made the uncomfortable ones difficult?
- How did each of these relate to the level of power?
- Did you have any choice about your level of comfort?
- What situations from your past might have impacted on your comfort level?

The cognitive behavioural framework, which has been used extensively for working with people with mental health issues and, more recently, has been expanded greatly to work with offenders, uses the triangle of behaviours, thoughts and feelings and how these inter-relate. Within the cognitive behavioural triangle sits our 'cognitive schemata' or story of the world – the way we were brought up, our individual characteristics, our community, our beliefs and values. These beliefs all affect how we see, interpret and respond to the world. Working with families who have views of the world which are unhelpful to them means that, as workers, we have to try to understand their story, start to unpick it and refocus and reframe the story, to offer a different story which still makes sense to them in their world.

The cognitive behavioural model works on the basis that thoughts, feelings and actions are inextricably linked, and if we change one it will have an effect on the others. As the above diagram suggests, our actions and behaviours are visible to all around us (above the waterline), whilst our thoughts and feelings are a much bigger part of who we are, but these are invisible and under the surface. Some approaches to cognitive behavioural therapy (CBT), work to change the behaviours that have an impact on the thoughts and feelings, whilst other approaches start with work on the thoughts and feelings to change the way that the person is thinking about themselves and their history, so that they can start to change their behaviours.

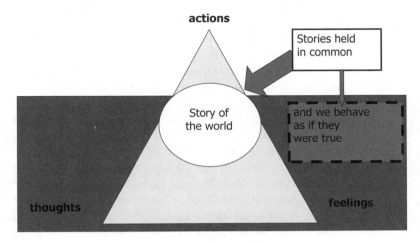

Figure 1.1 The Iceberg Model and the Story of the World

The behaviours, thoughts and feelings are all linked by the story of the world which we have in our heads, based on our family upbringing, our sense of community, our education, our peers, our experiences of how the world has treated us in our lives so far and all the external pressures around us. We then behave and respond to 'them', the other people around us, as though this story is the truth. These stories are strongest when they are based on belief systems which are held in common by a number of people, from a particular community, school, or social group.

Many service users' stories of the world is that they are not very 'worthy' people, that life is tough, that people in authority are against them and not to be trusted, and bad things always happen to them. The story which many young offenders hold in common is that violence is how everybody solves their problems, shops are all insured anyway so they don't lose anything and that they have a right to what 'everybody else' has.

Case study

After many years struggling to care for her two young daughters on her own, Sally eventually insisted the local authority look after Ava, her oldest child, who is severely disabled. Sally refused to consider foster care for her daughter and threatened to sue the local authority if they insisted on moving Ava from the short-break unit where she had been placed in an emergency.

Successive social workers said they found Sally confrontational and difficult to work with. She became unpopular with staff in the short-break unit, constantly correcting them and insisting she administer the enema Ava needed regularly rather than allow staff do it.

Eventually a social worker was able to make a trusting relationship with Sally, enabling her to confide her childhood experience of being repeatedly raped by her stepfather and her feelings of guilt at her previous partner's abuse of Ava, which had caused her impairment. She was also able to talk about her negative feelings about disabled people, arising from a frightening incident as a young child. These experiences combined and led to her belief that the only reason someone would volunteer to foster a disabled child was in order to sexually abuse them, hence her refusal to consider this option for her daughter.

It was the social worker's belief that Sally had reasons for her behaviour – her story of the world – and the social worker had the persistence to uncover what this was and how it was influencing Sally's behaviour and decision making. After that, it was possible to move on.

The work with service users can focus on either the actions/behaviours or the thoughts or the feelings, to start the change process. The work requires a focus on that person's particular story of the world, what they say about themselves, what they say about others and how they view you as a worker. This work often feels like gently picking at the edge of the story, to question the beliefs, and to try to understand the rationale for those beliefs. Subsequently, one can slowly start to show the service user that this is a particular view of the world, and that there can be others.

Points to consider

- If you had to describe your story of the world, what would you say about it?

- What influencing factors would you identify which have helped form your story?

- How might this act as a bias in your approaches to service users?

Prejudice

It is our story of the world which gives rise to our prejudices. There are many variants of the definition of prejudice, usually containing the following elements:

> An opinion formed beforehand, (without knowledge or on the basis of partial knowledge or selective use of knowledge) which is unlikely to alter, even in the face of contrary evidence.

or

> A pre-conceived preference or idea.

Our story of the world is developed from our personal histories, our experiences and our education, all of which contribute to how we see others. We all have prejudices against particular people and particular groups, depending on the circumstances and what any particular group represents to us. At work we try really hard to manage our prejudices in order to remain 'professional'; however, sometimes maintaining that stance is difficult and demanding and we need support.

There appear to be several reasons why prejudices persist. Obviously if we are socialised to particular attitudes it is more difficult to forget them. Although attitudes do change from generation to generation, we still remember the stories that our ancestors told us and these impact on our subconscious reactions to others.

Benevolent prejudice

> Benevolent prejudice is a superficially positive type of prejudice that is expressed in terms of apparently positive beliefs and emotional responses. Though this type of prejudice associates supposedly

good things with certain groups, it still has the result of keeping the group members in inferior positions in society. (Whitley and Kite 2010)

Believing a person needs a social worker or should be cared for by others because they are disabled is an example of benevolent prejudice. Although not overtly hostile, this view increases the likelihood that disabled people will be excluded from making decisions about their own lives, or they may be treated less favourably with regards to opportunity for advancement, because they are seen as less capable (Staniland 2009). There are also clear indications that perceptions of disabled people's vulnerability can play a role in their being targeted in crimes (Sin *et al.* 2009).

Task

Mrs Taylor, aged 85, lives alone and has a care package which includes three visits each day from support workers. Her granddaughter, Mrs Farmer, telephoned the duty manager to ask for a reassessment of her grandmother's needs and Philip, a student social worker, was allocated the task. Before visiting Mrs Taylor, Philip talked to a worker in the team who already knew the family; she told him that Mrs Farmer had been 'trying to have her grandmother put into a home for years,' but that Mrs Taylor wanted to 'stay put' in her own home. She implied Philip would need to be resolute in resisting this.

During the home visit to complete the assessment Mrs Farmer listed all the reasons why she felt her grandmother wasn't coping. Mrs Taylor didn't say much throughout the visit and it felt to Philip that Mrs Farmer was doing all the pushing, just as his colleague had predicted.

It was only later that Philip discovered Mrs Taylor had been turning away the support workers, saying she didn't need them as she could fend for herself. This was evidently not the case; she hadn't been eating regularly, often missed taking her medication and spent all night sitting in her chair when she couldn't get upstairs to bed. She talked about being lonely and scared. She had also recently left taps running in the bathroom which had caused a flood in the house, damaging a ceiling and ruining carpets and furniture.

What prejudices might be in play here?

- held by Mrs Taylor, about social workers and what they have to offer?

- held by Mrs Farmer, about social workers and what they should be doing?

- held by The previous social worker consulted by Philip, and her views on Mrs Farmer and Mrs Taylor?

- held by Philip, about all concerned?

Stereotypes

Stereotypes are shorthand for grouping people together based on particular characteristics. We can recognise the commonality of the group and some of the features that make them a group; dress style, approach to life, etc. We might be quite happy to accept that there are stereotypes of social workers or lawyers, for example; however, we find it more difficult to accept stereotypes of other groups, such as gay people, those who have mental health difficulties, or service users, particularly if they start to suggest negative connotations.

Points to consider

In a training exercise participants were asked if a social worker, doctor, health visitor and police officer were a household object, what would they be and why? This resulted in a lively debate which drew out many of the stereotypes commonly associated with these groups. Social workers, for instance, were portrayed as a laundry bin overflowing with dirty clothes, hopefully all going to be washed and aired then ready to wear again. The doctor was depicted as a computer, 'very knowledgeable but rather impersonal,' whilst a consultant paediatrician was a long case clock 'very ornamental but a bit "posh" for ordinary homes and actually only does the same job as a watch which takes up less space.'

Another version of the exercise used types of trees. In this one, police officers came out as oak trees, solid and dependable, 'you can hide and keep safe in their branches,' while social workers were weeping willows, 'all soft and pliable, changing direction with the wind and generally rather "wishy washy"'!!

- What stereotypes do you have about colleagues from different professions?

- What stereotypes might colleagues from different professions have about you?

- How might these affect you in multidisciplinary working?

Stereotypes can be useful as a means of making sense of information and decision making during the day. However, they can also be harmful as they may result in our only seeing the characteristics associated with the stereotype, rather than the whole person. So being labelled a prostitute, for instance, may result in the person being seen only as a sex worker, with all other aspects of their life and relationships being ignored. This has been particularly noticeable in media reporting of cases where women sex workers have been murdered. Many Youth Offending Team workers have baulked at the current trend of labelling their young people as 'offenders'. They may be young people who have committed offences, but they are much more than just an offender.

Stereotypes can cause us to assume that a widely held view is true when it may not be. They can lead to assumptions, which if left untested may lead to dangerous practice, for example, avoiding people with mental health conditions because we think they are prone to violence, even though this is not true. In his report into the death of Victoria Climbié, Laming (2003) commented on stereotypical assumptions which had affected practice in relation to Victoria, including an assumption about relationships in African-Caribbean families, and 'that children who have grown up in Africa may be expected to have more marks on their bodies than those who have been raised in Europe' (p.345). Another commonly held stereotype is that gypsies are dirty and leave their sites in a mess. Yet many gypsies live in immaculate, highly polished and ornately decorated caravans and care deeply that their living environment is clean and tidy.

Stereotypes may cause us to make an assumption about any one person based on the characteristics of a group, for example that because someone is disabled they must be vulnerable. Several recent research studies, such as Sin et al. (2009); Quarmby (2008); and Mencap (2007), have highlighted the numbers of disabled people who have experienced targeted violence and hostility, yet many disabled people are leading active and fulfilled lives and would not see themselves as at all vulnerable. There is also a media-encouraged stereotype that assumes a teenager will display problematic behaviour, creating the image of out-of-control 'hoodies'.

We can then behave as though the stereotype is true without checking it out; assuming all fathers play less of a role in the upbringing of their children than mothers, having a disabled child is a burden, or an adult daughter living near to ageing parents will undertake a caring role. This may be particularly true as stereotypes are influenced by the setting in which they are occurring. Social workers may not hold these stereotypes about their friends, colleagues or neighbours, but slip into them in a work environment.

Case study

I am young and black with five children, and a social worker come round and made the assumption that the children all had different fathers. She was then surprised when they didn't. She just kept putting her foot in it and didn't even realise it! (Wiffin 2010, p.32)

A stereotype can be a self-fulfilling prophecy; people may only behave in a particular way to live up to the stereotype, for example gay men are 'camp' because the existing stereotype has suggested to them that this is an appropriate way to behave, but that negates the possibility that the person really does have these characteristics and the stereotype fits them.

Some people may adopt characteristics that conform to a stereotype in order to convey something about themselves or what they would like others to believe about them; people who shave their heads and display tattoos in order to put across the message that they are tough, for instance. Others may dress in a stereotypical way to communicate a message about themselves, dressing provocatively to suggest sexual prowess perhaps, or 'power dressing' to appear confident and capable. Of course, these inferences may or may not be true!

Stereotypes, particularly negative ones, are resistant to change, even when there is clear evidence which is in conflict with the stereotype. An obvious example of this was Margaret Thatcher, who despite her behaviour as Prime Minister, failed to change many people's perceptions of women's capabilities in senior positions, because she was categorised as an honorary man.

Stereotypes to consider

- Scots are mean.
- Overweight people are lazy.

- Redheads have fiery tempers.

- Mothers-in-law are scary and interfering.

- Blonde-haired women from Essex are dim.

- Rottweilers (or their owners) are vicious.

- Caribbean people are poor time keepers.

1. What is your response to the stereotypes above?

2. Do some make you react more than others? If so – why do you think this is?

3. What stereotypes make you angry and why?

Many of these stereotypes remain in common usage and can be called up as the basis for many a bad joke, despite any number of individuals who do not fit it.

There are ways of changing stereotypes. A study reported in the *British Journal of Social Psychology* (Haslam *et al.* 1996) discussed 'referent information influence'. This is where people are motivated to agree with the beliefs of other members of their groups, so if somebody from within the group suggests an alternative to a stereotype which the majority appear to agree with, then people will start to shift their stereotypes towards what they regard as the norm for the group.

Points to consider

- What stereotypes do you have about individuals or groups?

- What are your first thoughts when you hear about the following:
  - people on benefits
  - divorcees
  - asylum seekers
  - long-term unemployed.

- How might these stereotypical beliefs affect you in your work role?

There is a reminder of how important all of this is in the Assessment Framework for Children (Department of Health, Department for

Education and Employment, and Home Office 2000, para 2.29, p.26–27) which says that workers need to avoid:

- using one set of cultural assumptions and stereotypes to understand the child and family's circumstances

- insensitivity to racial and cultural variations within groups and between individuals

- making unreasoned assumptions without evidence

- failing to take account of experiences of any discrimination in an individual's response to public services

- failing to take account of the barriers which prevent the social integration of families with disabled members

- attaching meaning to information without confirming the interpretation with the child and family members.

Political correctness

Does this really exist? This is one of the phrases that get thrown around, usually in a negative or derogatory tone, implying criticism of the use of particular language or behaviour, or the suggestion that particular language should not be used.

There are two components to 'political correctness'.

Language gets labelled as 'politically correct', often because the person using the term does not see that particular use of language as necessary *from their perspective*. Changing words, or receiving advice not to use particular phrases, is seen as trivial, unnecessary or pedantic. Sometimes this might indeed be the case, but often there are good reasons why some language should not be used, and it is having that sensitivity *from the other person's point of view* that is important.

For example: some people get upset about the use of the term 'black' being applied to anything negative; for example, when the pound was forced out of the European Monetary System it was known as Black Wednesday. Yet financially, when we are 'in the black' we are in credit, and our finances are all right; it is when we are 'in the red' that we are in financial difficulty. So why was it not Red Wednesday? But other people do not necessarily see the use of black meaning negative as important. Whether it is or is not, it is the person's perception that is important.

Another more light-hearted example is where the supporters of one football club call the supporters of another 'dingles'. When first hearing the term, without having any knowledge of its origins or connotations, it seems quite sweet and innocuous. It comes from the television series Emmerdale, and refers to a particular family in a not very flattering manner. It is only in context that it can be appreciated as being derogatory and definitely an insult. This has come to be particularly relevant in the use of the term 'Paki'. Many people would still argue that it is only being used as a description of people coming from Pakistan. However, the extensive derogatory use of the term means that is can never be experienced as being neutral, and always has that negative connotation.

Another example is a phrase in use currently by some groups of people, 'that's so gay' to describe something useless, faulty or negative. Some would see this as innocuous, however, many people would consider it homophobic, demeaning and offensive.

The language used when referring to disabled people also illustrates this well. Many of the terms used in the past to describe people who have particular impairments later became used by some as insults, for example, 'you're such a retard' or 'you spaz'. We can hear disablist language on a daily basis – 'that's so lame' being used to describe something that is negative or useless, for example, or 'that's so short-sighted of you', 'turning a deaf ear/blind eye', 'what's wrong with him or her', all of which refer to disability in a negative way. In challenging such language we can be accused of being too sensitive; however, language is important in highlighting feelings about difference, including unconscious feelings. Being exposed to disablist language regularly can devalue the lives or experiences of disabled people with negative consequences for both disabled and non-disabled people in society.

The other use of political correctness is blaming a nebulous 'they' as responsible for banning the use of a word or phrase. 'They' say we can't talk about black coffee, or sing 'Baa baa black sheep'. A big issue for staff in organisations are beliefs about what can or cannot be said. Language is a social construct and dynamic; this would suggest workers need to be alert as to what language is currently acceptable, to whom and in what circumstances, as what is acceptable may be evolving. What is not politically correct from one person's perspective may well be from another person's viewpoint, and this may change over time. This would encourage workers to explore what is and is not acceptable to others through discussion rather than by rule.

An example of this is the tendency to talk about 'winter lights' for what has been called traditionally Christmas lights; some people see this as excessive political correctness, as it feels to them as if it is a denial of the Christian celebrations. If this is indeed the case, then it may well be politically correct, but if it was done as a wish for inclusivity, to include other religious celebrations such as the Jewish feast of Chanukah, then it may be an appropriate use of words.

Quite often we do not know very much about the society in which we live. We survive on half-truths which we gather from the media, much of which is written to provoke a reaction, or those around us, and 'common knowledge' which may or may not be accurate.

Points to consider

- How do you respond when somebody accuses you of only saying or doing something because of 'political correctness'?
- How can you justify yourself without becoming defensive?
- In what situations might you find it more difficult to give a measured response?

To conclude

Diversity is a complex and emotive subject, so it is important to gain knowledge of oneself and confidence to explore a range of differences openly and without getting defensive or unable to apologise if you have 'put your foot in it'. This chapter has provided a context for current social work practice and introduced the foundations on which the models that follow will build. As Thompson (2006) expresses so powerfully:

> Practice which does not take account of oppression, and the discrimination which gives rise to it, cannot be seen as good practice, no matter how high standards may be in other respects. For example, an...intervention with a disabled person which fails to recognise the marginalised position of disabled people in society runs the risk of doing the client more of disservice than a service'.
> (p.15)

Issues from this chapter to discuss with your supervisor

- Which of your own personal characteristics are important for you to be taken into consideration for you as a social worker?

- What aspects of your story of the world impact on your approach to your work?

- Your attitude to power and how you exercise it as a social worker.

- What prejudices and stereotypes you carry which may usefully be explored.

Further reading and resources

Bower, M. (1996) *The Will to Manage: Corporate Success Through Programmed Management*. New York, NY: McGraw-Hill

Department of Health (2010) *A Vision for Adult Social Care*. London: DoH.

Home Office (2000) *The McPherson Report into the Death of Stephen Lawrence*. London: HMSO.

Howe, D. (1993) *On Being a Client: Understanding the Process of Counselling and Psychotherapy*. London: Sage.

Howe, D. (2008) *The Emotionally Intelligent Social Worker*. Basingstoke: Palgrave Macmillan.

International Federation of Social Workers website (2004) Ethics in Social Work, Statement of Principles. London: IFSW.

Jandt, F.E. (2001) *Intercultural Communication*. Thousand Oaks, CA: Sage.

Lago, C. (in collaboration with Thompson, J.) (1996) *Race, Culture and Counselling*. Philadelphia: Open University Press.

Laming, H. (2009) *The Protection of Children in England: A Progress Report*. London: HMSO.

McGuire, J. (ed.) (1995) *What Works: Reducing Reoffending Guidelines from Research and Practice*. Chichester: Wiley.

McPherson, W. (1999) *The Stephen Lawrence Inquiry*, Cm 4262. London: Stationery Office.

Thompson, N. (2003) *Promoting Equality: Challenging Discrimination and Oppression*. London: Palgrave Macmillan.

Thompson, N. (2011) *Promoting Equality: Working with Diversity and Difference*. Basingstoke: Palgrave Macmillan.

Wiffin, J. (2010) *Family Perspectives on Safeguarding and on Relationships with Children's Services*. London: Office of the Children's Commissioner.

CHAPTER 2

A Model for Understanding Discrimination

Key messages

- Oppressive behaviour and language can have very different motivations and these are often not recognised.

- Understanding these motivations enables us to select the most appropriate response.

- It is important to recognise why behaviour and language might be perceived as offensive by others.

Introduction

The discussion about diversity has been led, historically, by gender and race. For the authors, race has been the 'front line' in identifying the impact of discrimination against and between people. In recent years, following the implementation of human rights legislation in Britain, other forms of discrimination have begun to receive more attention. The authors have found that a model developed with colleagues to explore the complexities of racism and to help professionals understand how racism manifests itself in society and in their own organisations can be applied to other forms of discrimination. The model works better for some forms of discrimination than others, but can helpfully be applied to all. This chapter will therefore start with the exploration of racism and then move on to the other subjects.

Race is often an area of great concern to social workers. Practitioners have felt uncertain and lacking in confidence when working with people from other cultures and racial groups, and this has shown itself through a range of reactions. A worker may be reluctant to challenge a statement made by a service user from an ethnic minority, partly because they fear that they will display ignorance about that culture, and partly because they are anxious not to damage the working relationship. In discussing diversity in any professional social care setting, staff will express uncertainty and discomfort in discussions about race, although other subjects with which they are more comfortable such as gender (still) and disability raise many of the same issues.

One common difficulty has been the use of language. 'We're not allowed to say that any more'; 'I don't know what I can say, so I don't say anything'; or 'Whatever I say I get it wrong'; are the sorts of things said in private between workers when talking about race. In the past there have been similar language taboos in relation to gender, and often feminism was blamed for the 'we can't say that' syndrome. Although uncomfortable at the time, these perceived language taboos did lead to helpful discussion and debate, and eventually to learning and development in our understanding about the importance of language in influencing behaviour.

Part of the difficulty for many people is the way in which inappropriate comments are perceived and interpreted by others, the manner in which they are challenged, and how to reach a successful resolution. Quite often the reaction to any accusation of racism is, 'I only said...,' and the comment itself might appear to many people to be quite innocuous. Sometimes the situation unfolds to show that although this might be a one-off 'only said' for the person who made the comment, for the recipient there may have been many experiences of people 'only saying' that comment. So what might have been laughed off or overlooked now becomes impossible to ignore. Many of us can cope with teasing for a while, but when the tease is repeated we become increasingly sensitive and finally react. If the person we react to is only saying this for the first time they are completely unsettled and unprepared for the reaction to their (as they see it) minor comment. Another dilemma is that what is acceptable to some people is completely unacceptable, even inflammatory, to others so the reaction is, 'Well, how could I know that they would be sensitive to that?'

Points to consider

- Is there an aspect of your life that you are or have been teased about that can make you feel very defensive?

- What makes the difference to you between acceptable and unacceptable teasing?

- How might you explain this tipping point to other people?

Because language is socially constructed, terms become more or less acceptable at different times. People born in the 1920s and 1930s, both black and white, were quite happy with the use of the term 'coloured' to describe black people. Black people of that generation have said that because this was so much more acceptable as a term than most of the names they had been called, it was perceived by them as being polite. But younger black people will say very firmly that their skin is not 'coloured' so the term is unacceptable. So the default position in the working environment has been that many workers who worry about getting it wrong say nothing for fear of being seen as racist. The term currently in common use is 'black and minority ethnic', frequently abbreviated to BME, but the use of this is still fraught with difficulties, is not universally accepted and sometimes feels like the least bad option.

Racism

Racism, a set of beliefs in which some people are deemed to be superior to others due to their race, has been usefully defined more fully as:

> ...a social construction, a way of making sense of the world by dividing people into assumed biological categories. However, these categories are not seen as neutral or value-free. What we encounter instead is a hierarchy of racial groups in which white groups are presented as superior to black groups (Pilkington 2003). And it is this notion that introduces racism, the systematic oppression of certain groups through processes of discrimination that occur at the P, C and S levels. (Thompson 2011, p.104)

The P, C, S model is explained in Chapter 1 and fully described in Thompson's (1998, 2001, 2011) books.

People have very different interpretations of the words 'racist' and 'racism' and respond emotively to their use. In law 'race' comprises colour, culture, ethnicity, and nationality. In a now well-known quote in the HMIP Inspection, of the Probation Service 'Towards Race Equality' (2000, para 13.21, p.142), one member of staff spoke for many in describing being called racist as 'worse than being called incompetent', confirming the seriousness with which that label is experienced.

In practice, at least three distinct dimensions have been identified: legal, ideological and cultural. A model which explains the inter-relationship between these three dimensions has been developed by Conroy Grizzle (unpublished). It has been used in training many hundreds of staff, particularly in the probation service, but also in other public and private sector organisations, and practitioners report that it helps with understanding the situations that can arise and how to work effectively with colleagues and service users.

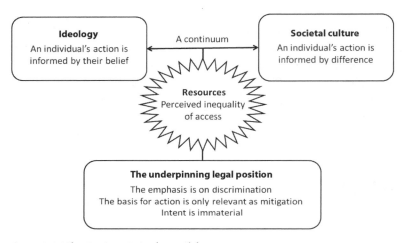

Figure 2.1 The Conroy Grizzle Model

The underpinning legal position

The first dimension is the law. The aim of all equality legislation is to achieve fairness. In dealing with a claim of racism neither the courts, in the case of racially aggravated offences, nor the employment tribunal, in the case of a workplace matter, are interested in the intention behind the behaviour or alleged comments. The simple approach that is taken is, 'did you say/do it or did you not?' The intent behind the action only becomes of interest at the time of decision making when it becomes a matter of mitigation. The key term in the legislation is discrimination.

Discrimination

Discrimination is the base line in legislation so it is helpful to be clear about the different terms used, their definitions and their meaning in practice.

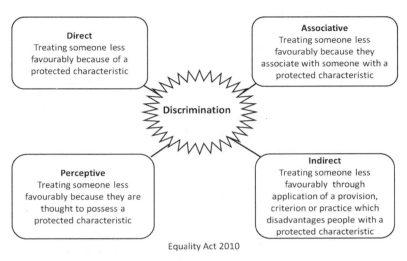

Figure 2.2 Understanding discrimination

Direct discrimination

The act describes direct discrimination as treating someone less favourably than another person because of a protected characteristic they have. These were identified in Chapter 1. Direct discrimination is unlawful under all anti-discrimination law. The legislation, which previously covered race, disability and sex separately, had been extended to cover religion or belief, sexual orientation, age and gender reassignment, and has now been extended to cover pregnancy and maternity.

Associative discrimination

Associative discrimination is direct discrimination against someone because they associate with another person who possesses a protected characteristic. For example, a member of staff is denied promotion because her mother has recently had a stroke and the organisation assumes that she will therefore have less time to concentrate on the job due to her caring responsibilities for her mother. This may be associative discrimination against her because of her association with a person with a disability.

Perceptive discrimination

Perceptive discrimination is direct discrimination against an individual because others think they possess a particular protected characteristic. It applies even if the person does not actually possess that characteristic. For example, an experienced member of staff who looks much younger than his years is not allowed to represent the organisation at a high level conference because he is thought to look too young to have the relevant experience. He has been discriminated against on the perception of a protected characteristic.

Indirect discrimination

This occurs where someone is treated less favourably through application of a condition, rule, policy or even a practice that applies to everybody but which particularly disadvantages people who share a protected characteristic. For example, requiring job applicants to have a set number of years' experience may indirectly discriminate against women who have taken a career break.

There are three issues with these definitions: who is protected, the need for a comparator and occupational requirements.

1. UNDER THE LAW ONLY THE PEOPLE HAVING THE PROTECTED CHARACTERISTICS HAVE LEGAL PROTECTION (EXCEPT BY ASSOCIATION OR BY PERCEPTION – SEE BELOW).

Employers can and do discriminate all the time, for example, choosing people with more of a particular type of experience, but they cannot choose an older person rather than a younger one (discrimination on the grounds of age) without being clear that they are making the choice based on the level of experience, not age.

Discrimination in itself is not unlawful, except for these protected groups. However, if the policy of a particular organisation lists other protected groups, then they have protection too. This has sometimes included protection for people who are members of trades unions. However, some organisations have included the phrase 'or on any other improper grounds' which, whilst this might be very well-meaning, leaves them open to be 'hostages to fortune', as there would have to be a full exploration of what constitutes an improper ground if challenged.

Points to consider

- What is included in your agency's equal opportunities or diversity policy?

- How would someone new to your agency experience these in their introduction to practice?

- How do the policies impact on your day-to-day work?

2. THERE HAS TO BE A COMPARATOR; THE ORGANISATION HAS TO HAVE TREATED SOMEBODY LESS FAVOURABLY THAN SOMEBODY ELSE.

The burden of proof for employment tribunals has now changed to the organisation having to prove that discrimination did not happen, rather than the employee proving that it did, and this means they have to provide their comparators. One organisation won an employment tribunal taken by a black woman for race discrimination on the grounds that they were not treating her less favourably than anyone else. They treat all their staff this badly!

3. THERE HAS TO BE AN OCCUPATIONAL REQUIREMENT.

This is very important because, in strictly limited situations, each piece of anti-discrimination legislation allows for a job to be restricted to a person within the protected characteristic group where it can be shown that this discrimination is necessary. An example might be seeking to employ a female member of staff to work at a women's refuge for women fleeing from domestic abuse, or seeking somebody who speaks a particular language.

An organisation has to be careful when identifying an occupational requirement, as it will always be open to challenge. An occupational requirement will be strictly interpreted by a tribunal as it derogates from the usual principle of non-discrimination, and it will be up to the organisation to prove the requirement, which is usually only permissible in very limited circumstances.

Positive discrimination is another term which can cause confusion. Positive discrimination was illegal in mainland UK until the introduction of the 2010 Act, and the new situation has yet to be tested in law. Positive discrimination was where an advantage was given, for example a job was offered, because of a person's race, gender, religion, sexuality, etc., and the discrimination was not based on a genuine occupational requirement. The law now states that if two people are exactly equal in a recruitment process then the employer can select the person from an under-represented group, although how this will work is yet to be tested in court.

Positive discrimination implies a policy or practice which positively favours an individual from an under-represented group. Many workers believe that quota systems exist and that certain people only got their jobs because they were from an under-represented group. This frequently leads to resentment against the person.

Although the specific use of discrimination relates to employment law, it has the same impact on the delivery of service. Was a service user treated less favourably because of a prejudice relating to one of the protected characteristics, in which case they have been the subject of discrimination? With a genuine understanding of this term practitioners can be much more confident about dealing with challenges of discrimination. It allows practitioners to ask themselves, 'Did I deal with this service user differently from other service users who I work with because of any particular characteristic?'

In practice

In returning to comments that are made or behaviours that occur, what happens both in employment law and criminal law is that if a person who is investigated for making an inappropriate remark or behaviour is challenged, and they admit that they did say or do it or are found to have said or done it, the presiding panel or court may then declare that this is racist. The person charged will then usually wish to deny that they were 'racist', claiming in mitigation, 'I only said/did…' This then falls into the 'fundamental attribution error' category (Munro 2008), which explains other people's behaviours as due to internal personality traits, whilst our own behaviours are due to environmental factors. Those judging believe that there is an error in attitudes and beliefs in the individual that needs addressing, whilst the person accused believes that circumstances of the incident – incitement, provocation or dis-inhibition – means that their behaviour was justified in these particular circumstances.

The legislation, however, is not interested in the motivation of the person being challenged. It only seeks to address the actual behaviours at the time of the offence. It therefore does not differentiate between the societal attitudes which get expressed, and the ideological attitudes which are often covert.

The person accused may well accept their actions occurred but cannot accept the label which is placed on them as a result of those actions, because of the underpinning messages implied by the label. Exploring the model further can allow us to see the different meanings of the word 'racist' and why it is received so badly.

Points to consider

There was evidence in the data that racist attitudes and racist behaviours towards IRN's (internationally recruited nurses) were motivated by racist beliefs about skin colour, ethnicity and nationality. This suggests that the relationship between racist ideology and the individual's prejudice needs further investigation, as it does not seem sufficient to argue either that racist ideology alone produces social exclusion and discrimination, or that racist individuals are responsible for racism within institutions. (Allen *et al.* 2004)

- How far do you think this also applies to internationally recruited social workers?

- What factors do you think influence attitudes to those recruited from overseas?

- What do you think the impact would be on social workers recruited from overseas? What do you think they would say about their experiences?

Ideological

Returning to the model, at the ideological end of the societal–ideological continuum are those people who have a well thought-out belief system, whereby one group of people are seen as superior to another, which guides their behaviour. In the recent past at a national level these beliefs have been acted out around race in Nazi Germany, due to a belief in the superiority of the Aryan race. Their interpretation of that term meant a non-Jewish Caucasian, especially of a Nordic type, who was meant to be part of a master race. These peoples were believed to be inherently superior to non-Aryans, by which they meant specifically, in a European context, Jews and Roma people.

In South Africa, with the policy of apartheid, and in a more localised way in the US, with the segregation of black and white people in the southern states, the belief was about the superiority of whiteness. The lighter skinned you were the more superior you were. This gives rise to the use of the term 'coloured', which in South Africa was applied to people of mixed (white) European and African (black) or Asian ancestry. The term has become to be viewed as offensive in the UK, but for a generation living in Britain during the Second World War, both black and white, it was the favoured term, with many black people preferring it to the other terms which were likely to be used about them. The superiority of whiteness is still embedded in many national psyches; despite the European ideal of a good tan, skin whitening is active and practised in many parts of Africa, in India, China and the Caribbean.

In the UK there are pockets of racial ideology: in the National Front, British National Party and more recently the English Nationalist Alliance and the English Defence League. Their belief systems, which often attract attention in the media, can seep into the societal attitudes of more people than those who would espouse the ideology. Offenders such as David Copeland, who in 1999 nail-bombed the Admiral Duncan pub in Soho, London, act out these beliefs, targeting black people (and in his case, gay people too) very specifically.

Most minority ethnic people who understand this model will accept that they have met very few ideological racists during their lives, but when they do meet one it causes intense discomfort. However, to workers engaging with some of the most disenfranchised members of society, it may well become apparent that some service users have bought into the ideology. Supervisors need to recognise the inherent dangers of a minority ethnic member of staff going out to do a visit in an area where there are known racial tensions, and trying to engage with service users on sensitive issues such as child protection, and how the worker is then uniquely vulnerable purely because of the colour of their skin. However, reactions motivated by attitudes about race can happen at any time, in any circumstances and are all the more shocking when unexpected.

Points to consider

- Why do people go along with ideologies (e.g. apartheid or the Nazi regime)?

- How difficult would it have been to stand out against those belief systems?

- How have both of these ideologies left their mark on current approaches to 'others'?

Societal

The belief underpinning the societal dimension is that people are basically tribal, and our tribe are okay, and 'they', another tribe, whoever they may be, are not okay. 'They' can be the people in the next village, the next estate, the other school, the other team, or whatever marks them out as 'not us'. Individuals from 'there' may be all right and accepted, but 'they' as a group are not. They are a threat to us, and we feel better according to how we position ourselves in relation to them. Most people when asked can recollect the rivalry between schools and what pupils used to say about the children at the other school and, indeed, banter between the supporters of different football clubs.

The animosity between such groups may be quite superficial. In order to feel like one of us we have to be different from them, and that difference is often the most obvious one; they may be wearing the wrong football team shirt, dressing in a different style, or have a different skin colour. At the societal end of the continuum people have varying degrees of awareness of their attitudes to others. Most of the time people see themselves as non-racist, often saying 'I treat everyone the same', but when provoked by some sort of trigger can come out with racist language.

The well used phrase, 'I'm not racist...' often indicates that those people are 'only' reflecting their societal attitudes and would not buy into the separatist or supremacist beliefs of the ideologues. A racist is 'one of them', somebody who has accepted the ideology, 'I am just expressing the views of my community and friends.' The phrase 'one of my best friends is black' used to cause anxiety to trainers, workers and colleagues, but it is actually a good indicator that the person is more likely to be is at the societal end of the continuum. An ideological racist is very unlikely to have minority ethnic friends.

Points to consider

- Are there any groups which you may see as 'different', using the explanation of societal difference above – from a different part of the country, sports team, etc.?

- What are the sorts of things that are said about these differences (even if only in a jokey way)?

- How easy is it to go along with these comments/jokes?

- What moves this into being racism?

The continuum

Between the societal and ideological extremes there is likely to be a continuum along which people, because of their experiences and the nature of the environment in which they live, can move from the general societal attitudes about who 'we' are, into a more intolerant set of attitudes about people who are not like us, for whatever reason; and regimes can encourage or discourage this. In our present society, where a great deal of media attention is given to 'Islamic terrorists', 'bogus asylum seekers', 'illegal immigrants', and all nature of others who make 'us' unsafe, there is probably already a tendency for the attitudes of many people in the groups from which public services draw their users, to be shifting from the societal to the ideological end of this continuum.

Competition for resources

Unifying all three dimensions is the perception that, in circumstances where resources are perceived to be limited, there is little enough to go round for 'us' and 'they' are coming here and taking a share of resources; our jobs, our housing, our health service, to which they are not entitled. This perception is promulgated by stories repeated in the media and passed around in communities that immigrants to this country receive an unfair and undeserved allocation of, for example, social housing, benefits or access to health services. When immigration is a feature of political policy, and the control of numbers entering the country is a platform on which parties compete to outdo each other (e.g. the British Prime Minister in April 2011 talking about restricting immigration to tens of thousands rather than hundreds of thousands of people, whilst the Business Secretary pointed out the economic dangers of imposing a cap on immigration), some people feel fully justified in acting on their behalf and attacking immigrants.

Hate crime offending

The Crime and Disorder Act 1998 introduced the potential for offences to be racially aggravated and the Criminal Justice Act 2003 expanded this to cover religion, disability and sexual orientation. In England and Wales, if abusive language has been used at the time of the offence, this is legally the basis for a prosecution for a hate crime. Often racist or religiously abusive offences, including graffiti writing, are not a product of calculated hatred, but they still do have a profound and cumulative impact on victimised communities.

Many racially aggravated offences have resulted from commercial transactions: shops, restaurants, take-aways, taxi drivers, etc. as described by Court and Durrance in Greenwich and Lewisham (2008). There has been a difficulty in the transaction, and the offender has, for example, shouted an insult (skin colour being the most obvious one), using a term that is seen as acceptable within the perpetrator's own community, but which they know is not acceptable when being used as an insult. The perpetrator would have used whatever term they thought would be most abusive to whoever was involved in the transaction.

It is known that many of the ideological offenders are known to the police and probation service, but perpetrators of racially aggravated offences are usually astute enough not to use antagonistic language, which would provide evidence, at the time of the offending. The tendency has been to treat societal offenders as if they held an ideology, when frequently they are simply using common language, admittedly with the intent to insult, but without seriously thinking about the ideological attitudes underpinning that language. This is likely to be particularly true for most young offenders.

Other areas of difference

Although the legislation applies in the same way to the other protected characteristics, aspects of the model do not transfer exactly into the other areas of difference, but there are parallels which are worth exploring. It is important because it impacts on how workers perceive difference and the attitudes they are likely to encounter from service users, who may hold particular attitudes because they are mimicking common terminology used by the media, or because they have not thought about the subject in any depth.

Gender

Gender expectations vary from society to society, culture to culture, and over time, and attitudes and assumptions about gender roles are so deeply ingrained that they can be hard to recognise and highly resistant to change. 'Like ethnicity, gender is something that is deeply rooted in our understanding and experience of the world and therefore needs to be handled sensitively if we are to enable people to move away from oppressive gender relations' (Thompson 1998, p.98).

Case study

Louise had previously worked for the probation service and was now a social worker. She objected to being called 'a girl' in the working environment. 'At home I might be quite happy to be "one of the girls", but at work, over 30 years ago, I joined a predominantly male, middle-aged working environment where being called a girl quite definitely had the sense of "and don't you worry your pretty little head about this..." and was experienced as very patronising.'

- How do you react to this?

- Do you understand the different perspectives that are expressed here?

Some women, as they get older, might be happy with the expression of youthfulness implied by 'girl'. Others have never considered that it might be used in a patronising manner so see no problem with it. However, for many it is completely unacceptable.

It is more difficult to call attitudes to gender ideological, but misogyny is at the far end of the spectrum. It implies a hatred of women that is usually displayed in an intolerance of women in particular jobs, roles in society, and attitudes towards them. In its extreme form it is not expressed very often, but is implicit in the high incidence of domestic violence involving male violence against a female. There are incidences of same sex domestic violence and some of female on male, but it is often the underpinning attitudes about the inferiority of women, alongside remnants of the belief that a woman was part of a man's possessions, that perpetuate a moral code that facilitates men's control and abuse of women.

Different societies have different tolerances of women's behaviours so collectively will be perceived to be at different points of the ideological/misogyny–societal continuum. In some Muslim communities men and women lead very separate and prescribed lives. Gender expectations are specific and from outside can look restrictive. Western workers may have ambivalent feelings about respecting the values of these communities, yet disagree strongly with practices such as arranged marriages, women being required to adopt particular forms of dress, and restrictions on some behaviours such as going out alone or even driving. Western women, seeing the behaviours from their own perspective, will sometimes describe this as medieval and find it hard to believe that the women willingly comply with the requirements placed upon them. From this viewpoint the male behaviours may be described as misogynistic, which could lead to assumptions and bias in assessment of family lives, and tensions between the worker and the family. For example, a worker could believe that they should undertake work to empower the woman, yet she might be quite comfortable with her lifestyle and unwilling to change. This is explored further in Chapter 3 in relation to power distance and different responses to hierarchical power.

At the societal end, the social care professions are usually much more gender aware than British society as a whole, practising equal opportunities policies and procedures, and having more female employees than many occupations. Indeed, in some areas of the work employers are struggling to recruit enough men, although men are still likely to be over-represented at the top of those organisations. As with race, staff are unlikely to express overtly sexist views, but jokes are occasionally told that are demeaning to women, or expectations revealed about who makes the tea and does the washing up.

Points to consider 1

A research project conducted in an assessment and care management team working with older people found that differences in professional responses to female and male carers still persist. Male carers received a higher level of day and respite care compared to female carers, even when the males were caring for people with lower dependency needs and females were caring for people with intensive needs (Bywaters and Harris 1998).

In another study researchers found that statutory services were often delivered on the assumption that other family members, particularly daughters, should help in preference to the state. They found home help and auxiliaries to assist with bathing have been denied to, reduced or withdrawn from elderly people who have local relatives, particularly daughters, available (Qureshi and Walker 1989, p.30).

- Where would you put this on the spectrum from misogyny to societal?

- What impact might this have on assessment?

- What other implications are there for practice?

Points to consider 2

> I don't understand women who leave their children. I'm a mother and I'd lay down under a bus to stop my kids from coming to harm. How can a mother leave her children, it's just not natural. (Comment made to author)

In UK society women who leave children are viewed negatively. Even leaving a violent relationship is not condoned if the woman does not take the children with her, regardless of whether or not they are considered to be at risk from the perpetrator.

- What does this say about gender roles and expectations in UK society?
- What implications are there for practice?
- Can you think of other examples where gender assumptions play a key part in practice and service provision?
- How might you challenge these in your own practice?

Religion

Religious antagonisms are different. Many religions have a structured belief system which includes particular attitudes to those who are not part of that religion. People may be brought up with, or choose to adopt, their religious beliefs and in many ways this may look similar to having an ideology, a body of ideas on which they base their lifestyle. Societies differ in their willingness to allow religion to be practiced and in their tolerance of multiple religions co-existing. On the whole, believers in this country display 'societal' attitudes towards people of different religions, wishing to differentiate between people who are part of their own group and those who are not. There is a recognition of fundamental difference; the majority are happy to accommodate this, but a minority feel the need for radical action to change the beliefs of others, and inter-religious violence can and does break out.

At different times different religions have been subject to intolerant behaviours. The most obvious of these is the centuries of discrimination against Jewish people, which can still manifest itself from time to time, particularly in the form of graffiti on synagogues. More recently, of course, has been the growing antagonism towards people of the Muslim faith. Any offence where somebody has been targeted because of their religion is covered by the Criminal Justice Act 2003.

Many people in the caring professions will say that their own religious beliefs underpin their professional practice, and guide them in relationships with service users and colleagues. How much a worker should share openly in the workplace about their religious beliefs was in the past largely a matter of personal choice, but in recent years has become more of a contentious issue. One example of this was in the Victoria Climbié case, where the social worker's manager was criticised for discussing her religious beliefs in supervision (Laming 2003). Victoria's death also raised awareness of how a belief in possession, witchcraft or other spiritual and religious precepts could lead to children being abused, as this was found to be a contributing factor in her death.

The wearing of clothing and symbols relating to religion at work, or school, can also be controversial, as has been demonstrated by the increase in legal cases concerning religious dress and symbols over recent years, particularly in schools. Despite this the social work profession seems to have avoided having open discussion about what is visually acceptable and the impact that these symbols may have on service users.

Case study

Joanne, a social worker in her mid-20s, has been working with Kia, a 15-year-old who has complex needs. Kia has a troubled background; she has had bouts of anxiety and depression, has little support from her family and few friends, and often talks about feeling alone and hopeless. This has resonated with Joanne, as she too experienced similar feelings in her own teenage years. For Joanne the change came when she joined a local church and became a committed Christian. Her faith is now very important to her, she feels supported by it and more able to cope with life's challenges.

Kia sometimes talks about 'ending it all' and Joanne fears she might make another suicide attempt. Joanne dearly wants Kia to feel better about herself and her life, and would like to tell her about how her own faith has helped her to achieve this. She would like Kia to know that God is watching over her and cares about what happens to her, in the hope it might make Kia feel less alone and unloved.

- Do you think Joanne should talk to Kia about her beliefs?

- Are there factors 'for' and 'against' such a disclosure, and if so what are they?

- What would you do in a similar situation?

Sexual orientation

At the ideological end of the continuum the relationship between religion and homosexuality varies considerably, and is not always clear. Most faiths have views on bisexuality and homosexuality, many of which have changed over time, and the variation between denominations and individuals can be very wide ranging, from viewing homosexuality positively to discouraging or actively opposing it. Many religions distinguish between sexual orientation and sexual acts in terms of acceptance; even where they find the former acceptable the latter might not be.

Many Christians, for example, believe that their religion finds homosexuality unacceptable, and will acknowledge that they have a strong prejudice against homosexual people. The majority of these Christians, working in the helping professions, will accept that their own views are at odds with the legal situation, and would certainly not act on their prejudices and be discriminatory.

Points to consider

A court (2011) was reported as placing a foster parenting ban on a Christian couple because of their views on homosexuality. It was widely reported that the couple were told that laws protecting people from discrimination because of their sexual orientation 'should take precedence' over the right not to be discriminated against on religious grounds, despite the fact they had been described as kind and hospitable people who 'respond sensitively' to youngsters. The Christian Legal Centre 2011 reacted by saying that the judgement, 'sends out the clear message that orthodox Christian ethical beliefs are potentially harmful to children and that Christian parents with mainstream Christian views are not suitable to be considered as potential foster parents.'

- What are your views about whether they should have been allowed to foster or not?

- Why might you take that position?

- What do you think about one area of discrimination 'taking precedence' over another?

- What impact do you think reports like this have on the social work profession?

In fact the court appears to have withheld judgement on the grounds that they were not clear what they were being asked to pass judgement on, although the judges did express concern about the couple's attitude to homosexuality, their commitment to attend church twice on Sundays, when they were offering weekend respite care, and that they would not feel able to take a Muslim child to a mosque.

Different societies also display a range of attitudes towards homophobia. For example, a young man from a Roma family who realised that he was homosexual had to make a choice between remaining within the culture of his birth or maintaining his sexual orientation by living outside that culture. The two were completely incompatible, suggesting homophobia is at the ideological end of the spectrum for this group, as the young man may have risked losing his life if he came 'out' in his Roma community. A social worker with particular attitudes about homosexuality, working with this young man, might have conflicting values about helping him gain his independence from his community whilst at the same time have misgivings about him developing relationships within the gay community.

At times workers, as well as the general public, will make thoughtless comments about the gender of any one person's partner, assuming heterosexuality. This has encouraged people to continue to keep their sexual orientation hidden, so that the first openly homosexual rugby players and cricketers are only just being brave enough to 'out' themselves. It seems that the successful campaign 'Kick Racism Out of Football' is now being extended to sexual orientation, but is only really on the starting blocks. It is still an area which workers are anxious about addressing. This was illustrated well by a serious case review into abuse of children by their foster carers which noted workers had concerns about the care of the children, but were unwilling to bring them up for fear of being seen as prejudiced and homophobic (Parrptt, MacIver and

Thoburn 2007). It has also been suggested that gay men and lesbians are near the bottom of an 'unspoken hierarchy' of preferred foster carers and adoptive parents, often having to wait much longer than heterosexual couples for placements. (Community Care Live 2008). Birth parents too have been known to express a preference that their child should not be placed with homosexual parents, again creating a conundrum for the social worker, and potentially delaying placement. It may be that the societal attitudes towards homosexuality are currently already some way along the continuum towards having an ideological base, so there is more work to be done to address British homophobic tendencies.

Stonewall (1996, 2009) found that homosexual people are frequently targeted because of their sexual orientation and these offences are covered by the Criminal Justice Act 2003. However, there have been few prosecutions using this legislation.

Points to consider

- What were your parents' or family views about same sex relationships?
- What are your personal views?
- What has influenced your views?
- How might these impact on your practice?

Disability

The model is also helpful when considering disability. Beginning with the legislative dimension, the Equality Act 2010 replaced the Disability Discrimination Acts (DDA) 1995 and 2005, protecting anyone who has, or has had, a disability. So, for example, if a person has had a mental health condition in the past that met the Act's definition of disability and is harassed because of this, that would be unlawful.

The Act also protects people from being discriminated against and harassed because of a disability they do not personally have. For example, it protects people who are mistakenly perceived to be disabled. It also protects a person from being treated less favourably because they are linked or associated with a disabled person. For example, if the mother of a disabled child was refused service because of this association, that would be unlawful discrimination.

Disability hate crime remains almost invisible in official government statistics. Police forces have only been required to collect and report disability hate crime data in a standardised way since April 2008, and the Crown Prosecution Service (CPS) did not collect disability hate crime prosecution data separately prior to April 2007. Moreover, the CPS has admitted that the data it has collected since then has not always been reliable (Quarmby 2008).

Despite these difficulties and the lack of robust evidence comparing risks to disabled and non-disabled people, there is consensus in existing evidence that disabled people experience a heightened risk of violence and anti-social behaviour leading to victimisation, compared with non-disabled people (Sin *et al.* 2009). Added to this, targeted violence and hostility towards disabled people appears to be on the rise, although there is a significant gap between reported crime against disabled people and their experience as reported to researchers.

It was only when the Criminal Justice Act 2003 came into force that disability hate crime became recognised by the criminal justice system. Although Section 146 of the Act does not make hate crime a separate offence, it imposes a duty to increase the sentence for any offence aggravated by hostility towards the victim, based wholly or partly on their disability (or perceived disability). This demonstrates that motivation by hostility to a person, wholly or partly, on the grounds of disability or sexual orientation has been taken into account in sentencing, and seeks to give society a clear message that such crimes are wrong and will be taken seriously. It also allows courts to punish accordingly, as judges can impose greater sentences for these perpetrators.

Despite having these powers, many would argue the criminal courts do not always use them as effectively as they might. There have been a number of well-publicised cases where disabled people have been abused or killed and sentencing has appeared to be unjustifiably lenient. In the case of one autistic young person who experienced appalling physical abuse perpetrated by three 18-year-olds over several days, for instance, the sentence was 80 hours' unpaid community work and a three-month curfew (in Manchester, October 2010). It could be argued that the message this sent out to society was far from helpful; rather than highlighting the rights of disabled people and championing fair and equal treatment, it actually disregarded and devalued them.

Returning to the model this brings us to the ideological–societal continuum, and society's interpretations of disability. Different cultures and faiths have different views about disability, and in some these are extreme and disability may be seen as spirit possession. For instance, there are documented cases of child abuse linked to a belief in spirit possession involving children who have learning disabilities, mental health issues, epilepsy, autism, a stammer and deafness (DfES 2007).

It is true that in the UK societal attitudes towards disability have moved considerably over recent years, largely due to the efforts of disabled people themselves to raise awareness. However, the dominant group in any society produces ideas of normality, and categorises those who do not fit these norms as abnormal (Drake 1996). Many would maintain that the dominant view of disabled people in UK society today is still one of tragedy, abnormality and being less worthy of life. This dominant ideology is often expressed in media representations, or rather misrepresentations, of disabled people and their lives, adversely influencing the attitudes of others and propagating offensive stereotypes which categorise and objectify disabled people (Higgins and Swain 2010). 'Our disability frightens people. They don't want to think that this is something that might happen to them. So we become separated from common humanity, treated as fundamentally different and alien' (Morris 1991, p.192).

Moreover, Morris comments, '…it is the assumption that our lives are of such little worth, which we struggle against every day of our lives' (Morris 1991, p.192). In a situation where there is competition for resources, particularly as exists currently in health and social care, this is hugely important. A typical response is to put in place criteria and thresholds for access to services, and judgements are then made about who is 'entitled' and who is not. This can leave disabled people as being 'increasingly viewed as financial burdens' (Westcott and Cross 1996, p.14).

Perhaps nowhere is the impact of attitudes more evident than in the area of safeguarding disabled children. Most of the knowledge base used by practitioners working in child protection is built on the experiences of non-disabled children, and yet research indicates that disabled children are significantly more likely to experience physical, sexual, emotional abuse and neglect than non-disabled children (Cross, Kaye and Ratnofsky 1993; Sullivan and Knutson 1997). Over recent years the ecological model has been used extensively to understand the inequalities experienced by disabled children and how these can contribute to an increased incidence of abuse (Westcott and Cross 1996; Sobsey 1994; Wonnacott and Kennedy 2001). These inequalities are often supported by society's values and attitudes towards disabled children, alongside harmful myths and stereotyping, language that often demeans and devalues them, and an unwillingness to prioritise their welfare. These inequalities are often supported by society's values and attitudes towards disabled children, alongside harmful myths and stereotyping, language that often demeans and devalues them, and an unwillingness to prioritise their welfare. The statements in Table 2.1 exercise below are just some examples that illustrate this.

To illustrate this further, there is a lamentable absence of research on the abuse of disabled children and young people in the UK, and many would see this as a reflection of their devalued status in society. This is particularly noticeable in the field of sexual abuse, an area where there is a wealth of research and vast amounts of knowledge available to the practitioner, yet little of it addresses sexual abuse of disabled children. This remains a hugely under-researched area 'to the point of being dismissed' (Higgins and Swain 2010, p.55).

Table 2.1 Exercise

Statement	How would you counter the argument?
Disabled young people don't really want to have to choose – they'd rather have decisions made for them	
Most learning disabled people are not capable of making rational decisions	
Jokes about disabled people aren't offensive, they're just a bit of fun	
It's OK to have a disabled child in the club providing it's not detrimental to the other children	
It's against our club policy to allow disabled children without a helper being present	
We would make our facilities more accessible if only we had the money available to do so	
If you let people who have learning difficulties make choices they might choose to do things which are dangerous or risky	

Points to consider

Michael is 16. He has multiple impairments and needs help with all aspects of his life. Michael attends a special unit at the local high school and you have put in a support worker to help get him ready for school in the morning. Michael has an excess of saliva and tends to drool, so his mother always puts babies' bibs on him. Sometimes other children laugh at him and tease him about the bib. The support worker has seen cotton bandannas with plastic lining used for other young people who drool. She offered to make some for Michael, but his Mum said she doesn't think it matters. She says Michael doesn't know he's being teased and she just wants to keep his jersey dry.

- What do you think?

- How important is this issue for a teenager?

- How would you deal with having a different opinion from the family?

- Would you try to do something about it? If so, what would you do?

Class

Unlike the other issues discussed here class is not covered by legislation, although caste discrimination and harassment may be covered by the race and religious provisions of the Equality Act 2010 (Government Equalities Office Research Findings 2010/8). Neither is it explicitly mentioned in the National Occupational Standards, although poverty and social exclusion would imply class differences. Each person has a different tolerance to the class aspect of other people's backgrounds, depending on their own starting point. Although it is a subject not much discussed openly in Britain at the moment, attention to class difference increased after the 2010 general election with the large number of former public school boys in the government. Within the social care professions many older staff come from a self-defined working-class background, and are conscious of how their educational opportunities and greater social mobility have increased the possibilities for employment, home ownership, foreign holidays; opportunities which did not exist for their parents. Indeed there are a number of women working in social care who described to the authors how their grandmothers had been in service; their mothers had more opportunities mainly due to changes during the war, and who were then determined that their daughters 'made something of themselves', through education and employment.

In relation to the model, class has been an ideology, but not in Britain. The Hindu caste system, for example, is an ideology, whereby people are born into a particular caste, originally related to occupational status, and were expected to remain in that caste through marriage and all social contacts. Attempts are being made to remove caste barriers but, for example, there have been protests in Indian universities about the number of places allocated to 'dalits' – the untouchable caste – at the expense of those from higher castes who would normally expect to go to university. The similarity with Britain is that even though attempts are made to reduce class difference, attitudes about class remain, even if they are subconscious.

Generally in Britain class is a more insidious subject, therefore at the more societal end of the spectrum. Numerous serious case reviews have highlighted how all agencies involved were more likely to view in a positive light those families who were perceived to be more middle-class: comfortable, well-decorated home, well-educated and articulate and with an appearance of affluence. The values by which workers make judgements about service users' lifestyles are not always made explicit, nor explored in a way that identifies biases. It can be easy for teams of workers to become accepting of particular class-based standards and therefore less challenging of issues such as neglect, of children or the elderly, on the basis that this is normal for that housing estate or geographical area.

Case studies

> A lot of the judgements can be a class issue. In a lot of the big ones, like the case meetings, there can be people who don't even know the family members or the children (para 3.6, p.15).

> They have a view about you, they think just because you find reading and writing hard that you must be a bad parent (para 5.3, p.24).

> It's nearly always the poor people who have social worker involvement. The social workers don't seem to be trained to deal with poverty. They don't look at the problems created due to poverty, just are they good enough parents? They don't put it into perspective (para 5.4, p.25).

> (Wiffin 2010)

Points to consider

- How would you describe yourself in relation to class?
- What criteria are you using to make this decision?
- How might your service users perceive you in terms of class?
- What difference might this make in terms of how they relate to you?
- What visible aspects of class do you notice when you are working with service users?
- How might this affect your practice?

Case study

Paul was asked to undertake an assessment of a baby, whose father had previously abused his children during the breakdown of his relationship with the children's mother. The father, Graham, was now in a new relationship with a young woman with whom he had a baby daughter.

Paul looked up the address of the family and saw they lived on a large council estate which was notorious for having a high level of social problems, including alcohol misuse, drug taking and offending.

On arrival, the outside of the property looked very similar to its neighbours. There was a broken down car in the front garden, various bits of rusted garden furniture and some uncollected bags of rubbish. However, when Paul was invited in to the home he was surprised at how pristine it was; the living room was newly wallpapered, there were cream carpets and deep pile rugs on the floor, and he was asked to take his shoes off before coming in. When he came into the living room there was the sound of classical music playing in the background and the smell of scented candles. Graham offered Paul tea, which his wife served using a bone china tea service. Paul noticed certificates of achievement on the walls, along with some religious texts. During the conversation Graham explained to Paul that he had decided to 'start afresh' after his previous marriage had failed; he wanted to live a different kind of life and give his new baby daughter all the advantages she needed to get on. He said they'd already looked at private schools she might go to, and put her name down at one, he also hoped one day she would go to university. Paul was a little taken aback by the conversation, especially as he knew Graham had not been in work for some time and the family income was minimal.

In discussing the visit with his supervisor later, Paul commented that it was as though Graham and his wife had 'read up' on how middle-class people live and sought to recreate that in his home.

- What stereotypes might you have from the description of this household?

- If you had undertaken this visit, what aspects of the family's presentation might cause you anxiety and why?

- Why do you think that this case study has been included here?

The Code of Practice for Social Care Workers sets out the conduct that is expected of social care workers. This includes: 'declaring issues that might create conflicts of interest and making sure that they do not influence your judgement or practice' (General Social Care Council 2010, para 2.6, p.10) and stating workers must not 'discriminate unlawfully or unjustifiably against service users, carers or colleagues' (ibid. para 5.5, p.11) nor condone such discrimination by service users, carers or colleagues (para 5.6, ibid. p.11). Wherever beliefs, attitudes and biases come from, the most important requirement for workers in social care is to be alert to them. However, because many are socially constructed and implicit, they can be difficult to identify and articulate. A requirement on all workers is to review their values, explore how these are underpinned by societal attitudes, and challenge themselves to avoid bias in social work practice.

Conclusion

Treating people differently because of their primary characteristics has been commonplace for probably as long as people have been around, but there appears to be a difference between antagonisms about whether you are just not 'one of us', coming from a different tribe, community or background, and whether there is an entrenched belief that this difference makes you an inferior being and therefore can be treated accordingly. 'Social work is perhaps unique amongst professions in that it works largely with people who, in some way or another, are outsiders. Often, it is their very status as outsiders which brings them into contact with social work' (Doel and Shardlow 2005, p.215). Recognising and working with the experience of being an outsider does not include condoning behaviour against others perceived to be even more of an outsider. On a day-to-day basis, workers come across service users who express intolerant and unacceptable viewpoints. It is important that workers can challenge these viewpoints, explore the motivation behind attitudes and address the issues directly.

Issues from this chapter to discuss with your supervisor

1. Assuming your supervisor has not read this chapter, how would you explain the model to them?

2. What specific learning points are you going to take from this chapter to use in your social work practice?

3. Using the continuum between societal and ideological, how might you go about identifying where a person might be on any potential area of discrimination? How might this influence how you work with them?

Further reading and resources

Bowling, B. and Phillips, C. (2002) *Racism, Crime and Justice.* Harlow: Longman.

Chapman, T. and Hough, M. (1998) *Evidence Based Practice: A Guide to Effective Practice.* London: Home Office.

Fryer, P. (1984) *Staying Power: The History of Black People in Britain.* London: Pluto Press.

Hall, N. (2005) *Hate Crime.* Cullompton: Willan.

Marks, D. (1999) *Disability: Controversial Debates and Psychosocial Perspectives.* London: Routledge.

McDevitt, J., Levin, J. and Bennett, S. (2002) *Hate Crime Offenders: An Expanded Typology.* Washington, DC: The Society for the Psychological Study of Social Issues.

Middleton, L. (1999) *Disabled Children Challenging Social Exclusion.* Oxford: Wiley Blackwell.

Stonewall (1996) *Queer Bashing.* Stonewall. www.stonewall.org.uk

Tannen, D. (1989) *That's Not What I Meant.* London: Virago.

Tannen, D. (1995) *Talking From 9 to 5: Women and Men at Work.* London: Virago.

Tannen, D. (2001) *You Just Don't Understand: Men and Women in Conversation.* London: Virago.

Winder, R. (2004) *Bloody Foreigners: The Story of Immigration to Britain.* London: Little, Brown.

CHAPTER 3

Understanding and Responding to Cultural Diversity

Key messages

- We all view the world from our own national and organisational cultural perspective and this can distort how we view the behaviours of others.

- Although there are national and organisational cultural norms, each individual and family may or may not conform to these.

- Engagement with service users will be enhanced if workers can accurately respond to their cultural diversity.

Introduction

'We do not stop being cultural beings when we become professional. Rather, we layer our professional training onto our cultural selves' (Aronson Fontes 2005, p.8). This chapter explores variations in culture, both from different countries and within England, and how workers can recognise and respond to these.

Culture has long been recognised as a crucial component of how people make sense of their world, how they fit into the society around them, how they make sense of the organisation for which they work and how they assess the behaviours of others. It has a strong influence on expectations of self and others and how to behave in any given situation. Individuals are rarely conscious of their own culture and its impact on their story of the world, yet it affects practically every way in which the people of a group interact with each other and with outsiders. Nationality is a convenient method of identifying 'us' and 'them', but no national group shares a single dominant viewpoint. However, members of a nation do share a set of common experiences, themes and institutions which mould how they see the world. These include geography, climate, economic situation, racial mix, religion, language, political and government institutions, education system and approach to family life. Less tangible, but equally important, are the stories that people tell about themselves, the humour that is used, myths and metaphors.

Case study

Lloyd was born in Jamaica but came to England with his family when he was five. He grew up in an area where there were many West Indian families and absorbed much of that culture. When he goes to visit family members in Jamaica his behaviours identify him as somebody who grew up in England, yet in England he is definitely seen as West Indian, and with friends can happily speak in patois. In Spain, when he visits his wife's family, they identify his behavioural characteristics as typically English, which is not how Lloyd perceives his cultural identity.

- What behaviours do you think identify Lloyd as English or Jamaican?
- How do you think Lloyd identifies himself?
- How do you identify yourself?

Definitions

A famous definition of culture attributed to Peter Senge (1990) is 'the way we do things around here'. This suggests a set of norms, of which people may or may not be conscious, which impact on how they act. Hofstede (2001, p.21), in his extensive study, defined culture as 'the collective programme of the mind which distinguishes the members of one human group from another'.

- It is the taken for granted nature of culture that is most important in social work.
- Workers are likely to think that their way of doing things is normal.
- Their cultural influences impact on every interaction in their lives.
- People approach every interaction from their own cultural perspective and see others with cultural blinkers in place.

Social workers are almost inevitably practising across cultural groups. This might involve the obvious differences such as race or nationality, but it can equally include geographical location, encompassing regional variations, class, educational attainment and communication patterns, including accent, dialect and idiom. How workers and service users come across to each other will depend on their abilities to understand each other's cultural environments. For example, it has been traditional in many social care agencies to dress in a casual and low key way so as not to highlight differences in income, authority and power, yet many service users see this style as scruffy, disrespectful and disingenuous. However, a smart style of dress may also create difficulties: 'If you're on benefits you can't always afford to look good, as they do in the smart suits. How would you feel if someone was coming to your house all official?' (Wiffin 2010, para 3.4, p.13).

Cultural differences affect assessments, interpretation and analysis. Aronson Fontes (2005) points out:

> When I meet with a family with a background that is different from my own, I bring all my professional and personal lenses with me. How I see the family is determined in part by how they compare with what I have known previously: people in my family of origin, other families with whom I've worked, and cases I have heard about. As much as I might like to, I am unable to view this family with lenses other than my own. (Aronson Fontes 2005, p.7)

A front line worker may view asking a family to participate in a problem-solving exercise as a way to engage with them and make them feel more part of the decision making process. However, a service user who has been taught deference to age, gender or job role might, out of respect, shy away from offering suggestions to their worker, in the belief that to do so might be seen to be inappropriately challenging someone in authority.

Culture and communication

Culture and communication are closely linked. Culture as communication is the process of creating and using shared meanings within communities. We exist within a framework of shared meanings which are frequently taken for granted. There are different key ideas about culture as communication, highlighted by different theorists (see Guirdham 2005) but they all emphasise that language and communication draw people together, creating in-groups and out-groups, and cultures develop because people communicate more with their in-group and common language helps to glue people together.

Families have their own culture, their own style of living their lives: how they communicate, how much time they spend together, and how they respond to the outside world. Social workers are no different, and to communicate effectively the worker needs to be able to understand their own cultural drivers as well as those of others, in order to understand and relate to service users and their patterns of behaviour. It is all too easy to judge someone by the unconscious cultural norms that we apply to our own lives without realising that is what we are doing.

Organisations also have their own cultural communication styles, between members and when referring to others. Depending on where you practice, a teenage service user might be a child, a young person, an adolescent, a juvenile, a young carer or a young offender! These cultural communication structures and styles can be very powerful, and even after one day of 'work shadowing' it's noticeable that a student will have begun to adopt the language that is culturally accepted in that particular work setting.

However, what is helpful communication shorthand in one organisation can be problematic when working across different agencies. Problems in inter-professional communication have played a crucial part in child abuse tragedies over the years, and continue to do so in those most recently in the national headlines. As Reder, Duncan and Gray (1993) comment in their seminal work analysing more than 30 child deaths: 'Inter-professional communications are embedded within multiple relationship contexts and … during every professional interchange personal, professional, institutional and inter-agency factors colour how the messages are relayed and received' (Duncan *et al.* 1993, p.65).

Points to consider

A police officer and I had been working on a child protection enquiry all day. We had been communicating with each other well and it had all gone smoothly, particularly as the person who had allegedly abused the child admitted what they had done. I certainly hadn't noticed any differences in our communication style. Until we got back to office, that is. The police officer telephoned her line manager to bring her up to date with what had happened, and before my eyes, she suddenly seemed be speaking a different language, saying the abuser 'had coughed' and was 'singing like a budgie'! It reminded me more of television police dramas than my experience of working with her during the day. Then when she came off the telephone she reverted to how she had been talking all day! It was the first time I had really realised that two organisations can have different sets of internal communication patterns, yet also can adapt to communicate effectively with each other when working closely together. (Experience of one of the authors)

- What cultural communication norms exist in your agency?

- What impact might these differences in cultural communication have on working in a multi-agency setting?

- How might this impact on service users?

A model for understanding cultural differences – the work of Geert Hofstede

In the late 1960s and 1970s Hofstede undertook several comprehensive studies of organisational and national culture, based on work undertaken for IBM, which has useful messages for social work. The company was developing globally and trying to understand why American and British management techniques did not transpose to other countries, and the 'IBM way of doing things' was not working in some of their overseas establishments. It was a large survey (116,000 questionnaires) carried out in over 40 countries (Hofstede 2001, p.11).

From this research Hofstede identified four particular dimensions which differ across national cultures. He labelled the four dimensions for understanding cultural differences, which he called cultural lenses: power distance; uncertainty avoidance; masculinity; and individualism. Hofstede was very clear that no one view of the world was better than any other, but noted that each person tended to judge people more severely if their cultural view was opposed to their own. He was also clear that just because a particular country had a tendency for a position on each of the dimensions, there was no increased likelihood that any one person in that country would fit with their country's cultural norms. Within all cultures there is likely to be a wide variation in practice, with each individual in that society making choices about which aspect of their culture they adopt, and which they do not. Cultures are not static, 'people and cultures don't fit into neat little boxes'. (Harrison, Harvey and Maclean 2010 p.30). It is absolutely vital to recognise every individual as unique.

So assessing any individual because of their country of origin cannot be taken for granted – any one person may be anywhere along the normal distribution curve, either grouped around the norm or anywhere on either of the extremes.

Power distance

> A pet food manufacturer keeps 30 cats as a consumer panel. At the time of feeding, the cats queue up in a definite order, always the same. Only when a new cat enters is there some disorder. It tries to take a place in the queue and is bitten by every neighbour until it has found a place where henceforth it is tolerated. Similar orders of inequality expressed in 'dominance behaviour' have been found among chickens (hence the term 'pecking order' and among many other animals). (Hofstede 2001, p.79)

Power distance is the extent to which a stratification of society is accepted, where individuals are accorded different levels of importance and status. In a high power distance society there is a high differential in status, but this is not a matter of discomfort. All members of the society, including the less powerful, expect and accept that power is distributed unequally. In a high power distance society, those with power are expected to be able to give orders which will be followed without question. In the UK, higher power distance organisations include the military, where rank is accepted without question, with people of higher rank having the unquestioned authority to tell those of lower rank what to do and not to be questioned about it. Uprisings in North Africa and the Middle East in 2011 may be indicative that people who have previously been accepting of the power distance environment are now beginning to challenge it.

Case study

A Chief Probation Officer who had previously been a submarine commander found it very difficult when first working in the service. He would tell stories against himself and the learning he had to go through on joining a very different organisation, because his expectations were that when he told people to do something they would do it, yet in the Probation Service he was constantly being asked why. He had never had that before.

High power distance parents will expect to tell their children what to do and that it will be done – they might be perceived as authoritarian, demanding, rigid and uncaring. Children in a high power distance family will be socialised to do as they are told without question, as they are expected to know their place. How the authority is maintained will vary – in some families it will be purely on expectations and 'disappointment' if a child does deviate, yet in others power will be maintained in a more physical manner.

Case study

Hyacinth had been in her team for some time and was considered a manager's dream member of staff. She was hard working, conscientious and would always do what she was asked. She was well regarded by her colleagues, and seen as a good team player.

In due course she was promoted within the same team. As the manager she was experienced as authoritarian, bossy and unsympathetic. Because she was black, there were murmurings about the power going to her head and black people not being able to manage power.

In fact she hadn't changed. She was high power distance. As a team member she expected to be told what to do and would do it. As a team manager she expected to tell others what to do and that they would comply. However, the culture in her team was low power distance, so they responded to her according to their norms. A discussion using this model was able to acknowledge the reasons for the behaviours and start a process to discover how Hyacinth and the team could work together.

Low power distance is much more egalitarian: the boss is first amongst equals, and different grades of staff within organisations are likely to be on first name terms. In low power distance societies everything can be questioned, communication is direct and open, but there are indirect rules about how much disagreement can be allowed to be overt.

Parenting is likely to be informal, with parents seeing themselves as friends with their children and being called by their first names. Viewed from a high power distance perspective this might look like children having too much responsibility, power and control in their lives, and that they are insubordinate and 'should do as they are told'. In low power distance cultures there is a higher value placed on high independence than obedience, and from an earlier age, but cooperation is encouraged.

Points to consider

> We had a letter from the social services on a Friday night. It said they had had an anonymous call and they were coming around to visit on Tuesday at 9.00. Apart from being scared I thought I will be at school then. What am I going to do? What could I do? If I stayed in they would hold not going to the school against me, and if I was not there, they would think I was avoiding them. So many times you think, I can't win here. And you can't. (Wiffin 2010, para 3.2, p.11)

- What use was being made here of power distance?
- What differences in power distance can you detect between the social worker and the service user?

In terms of the French and Raven's (see Chapter 1) classification of power, there is more coercive and referent power used in high power distance cultures and more reward, legitimate and expert power used in low power distance cultures.

Points to consider

How comfortable are you with power distance?

Do you accept that a senior person in the organisation can tell you what to do, and you do it without question?

If yes:

- Do you expect service users to accept your advice and guidance without question?
- How do you regard a service user who is very challenging of your opinions?
- What indicators of respect do you expect from colleagues in other organisations?

If no:

- Do you get concerned if service users are following your advice without question?

- Do you feel uncomfortable if a service user is being very deferential?

- How do you feel when you are expected to be circumspect with senior members of the police, medical professions and legal professions?

Consequences for organisations

In inter-agency work it is important to recognise that some organisations are higher power distance than others, for example, the police and nursing professions are higher power distance than social care. Police services have a tendency towards a style of decision making that will be 'just tell them', and cannot see any difficulties with immediate implementation. Also, being high power distance, staff will be sent off to whatever duties are seen as most important at that moment, so for instance they can be withdrawn from inter-agency meetings at the last minute, which others will find frustrating, incomprehensible and maybe even rude. This has important implications for inter-agency working, and can get played out in, for example, Local Safeguarding Children Boards, when a police officer is 'sent' by a senior officer to represent the service, without any knowledge of the business or even knowing why they are there. 'Working with a team of senior managers in the police including the Chief Constable, he said – "we are all students here, so we can use first names" – to which the reply came immediately "Yes sir!"'.

So in terms of how organisations behave, it is important to understand the characteristics of the different dimension as they get played out:

Table 3.1 Comparison between low power and high power distance organisations

Low power distance	High power distance
Less centralisation	Greater centralisation
Flatter organisation pyramids	Tall organisation pyramids
Smaller proportion of supervisory personnel	Large proportion of supervisory personnel
Smaller wage differentials	Large wage differentials
High qualification of lower strata	Low qualification of lower strata
Manual work same status as clerical work	White collar jobs valued more that blue collar jobs

Based on Hofstede (2001).

This comparison highlights how the UK has shifted over the past 30 years. The national culture and certainly social care organisations have moved towards higher power distance. The public sector has moved towards greater centralisation and more hierarchical structures. Some social workers have found it difficult to accept the higher expectations of conformity, whilst many have accepted the requirement of obedience as a form of protection from blame if things go wrong.

Uncertainty avoidance

This term refers to the cultural differences which relate to ways of accepting and coping with uncertainty, ambiguity and risk. In the current political climate, how risk is managed in social work, and how it is perceived by the public, has been very high profile.

High uncertainty avoidance cultures like rules and regulations and are quite happy to follow them as it helps to contain their uncertainty. The expectation is that rules are there to be followed. In a high uncertainty avoidance family, children will be socialised to do as they are told without challenge and not make mistakes, not because it is an adult telling them (which would be high power distance) but because that is how everyone is kept safe. The family rules are likely to be explicit and deviation is not encouraged. The uncertainty of life is a continuous threat and all efforts must be taken to contain it. Levels of stress are high and anxiety is almost the norm. Children learn to copy what is around them to ensure that in time they become less likely to make an error.

Points to consider

The following are all quotations from service users:

> I have had loads of those assessments, you are asked the same questions, over and over, and it leads nowhere. And then out of the blue you are asked to attend a case conference. What's that all about? (para 6.4, p.33)

- Where would you place this service user and their social worker on an uncertainty avoidance scale?

- What explanation does the service user need about the procedures that are being followed?

- How could the social worker better engage with the service user around uncertainty avoidance?

I said to the social worker, 'I am too down today, can we make the appointment for another time?', and she said, 'No, I have to come today, it's the rules.' (para 6.5, p.34)

- What is the impact of the social worker's level of uncertainty avoidance on the service user?

- What explanation does the service user require to ensure they understand the uncertainty avoidance requirements?

My social worker had to go on leave after a year. Someone else took over. Two of my girls went into long-term foster care. The first social worker set it up for me to see the children in the summer holidays. The next put a block on it. When she left and another one came, because of what she had written, she had to follow it and so we weren't allowed to see the girls. It actually took the old social worker screaming at the other social worker to say they have a right to see their girls in the foster home.

(Wiffin 2010)

- How are the different levels of uncertainty avoidance of the social workers impacting on the service user?

- How does a service user make sense of the different approaches?

- What benefits would there be for the department to explore different approaches to uncertainty avoidance?

Low uncertainty avoidance cultures are happy with people thinking for themselves, having a go at things and learning from mistakes. Lower uncertainty avoidance cultures are often better at accepting outsiders, and encourage personal choice and decision making. Guidance will be minimal and as limited as possible, to allow exploration and creativity. Innovation is looked on more favourably in a low uncertainty avoidance culture than a high one. Every day is taken as it comes and the uncertainty of life is relatively easily accepted. Consequently there are lower levels of stress and a more easy going approach to life.

At the time of Hofstede's research, Great Britain was one of the lowest uncertainty avoidance countries, but most people would agree that this has shifted enormously over the past three decades. This is particularly noticeable in child protection, where the system of expecting staff to follow exact processes was developed with the intention of reducing the likelihood of child deaths. In interactions with service users, workers in the UK are still more likely to be more towards the low uncertainty avoidance end of the continuum, even though the organisations expect greater uncertainty avoidance from their staff than was the case a few years ago. The residual tendencies of lower uncertainty avoidance is likely to be a less explicit style and less directive language used in their communication with families, working through hints and suggestions rather than instructions. High uncertainty avoidance families would prefer explicit instructions and may be confused without them.

Case study

William worked in a disabled children's team, and prided himself on his ability to form and keep effective working relationships with parents. When a situation arose in one family that resulted in a child protection concern, William's supervisor instructed him to draw up a written agreement with the parents. William initially resisted this; he said he preferred to simply talk through the issues with the parents and thought having to do a formal written agreement with them would undermine the relationship he'd worked hard to establish, and be perceived by them as being punitive. However, later in his discussions with the parents William was surprised to find they welcomed the idea of a written agreement. They felt it would enable 'both sides' to be clear about what needed to change and the help they needed, who was to do what by when, and what would happen if someone didn't do what they were supposed to, or this didn't resolve the difficulties.

Points to consider

Rules, for instance, are a quick solution to minimise the chances of a social worker making an obvious mistake but rules, in a compliance culture, can lead to workers just doing as they are told and not learning why the rule is generally appropriate. This deeper understanding is needed to enable workers to respond to the varied circumstances of children and make judgments that a deviation from the rule is in the best interests of a specific child or young person. (Munro 2011a, s.4.67)

The final two weaknesses are interwoven: procedures can deal well with typical scenarios but not with unusual ones, and an organisational culture where procedural compliance is dominant can stifle the development of expertise. In child and family social work, the needs and circumstances of children are so varied that procedures cannot fully encompass that variety. Efforts to make procedures cover more variety quickly lead to the proliferation of procedural manuals that, because of their size, become harder to use in daily practice. The inquiry into the death of Victoria Climbié found that there were 13 documents containing policies, procedures and guidance to staff in relation to child services. Dealing with the variety of need is better achieved by social workers understanding the underlying principles of good practice and developing the expertise to apply them, taking account of the specifics of each child's case. The work of Dreyfus and Dreyfus (1986) on how people develop expertise shows how they build up intuitive understanding and tacit knowledge. They may use procedures to get started as novices but need to move beyond this to achieve mastery. Social workers in a culture where procedural compliance is expected, and deviation is met with blame, are discouraged from building up that expertise. (Munro 2011a, s.4.42)

- How does this reflect your recent experience in your current work setting?

- Do differences in uncertainty avoidance create any tensions for you in your own organisation or in inter-agency work?

Staff who have been around for several years were probably appointed at a time when low uncertainty avoidance was the norm, so may find it more restrictive to be 'hide bound' by policies and procedures. They may have started their practice at a time when monitoring was limited, use of assessment tools was optional and flexibility was valued. These staff now resent the time required to sit in front of a computer and complete the assessment and recording procedures, as these feel restrictive and limiting. However, more recent recruits are more likely to have been appointed with a higher uncertainty avoidance preference or trained into such an approach, so are more relaxed with a structured and procedural way of working. It will not feel prescriptive to them and they feel that both they as workers and the services users are receiving a better service because their safety is being protected.

Points to consider

- How comfortable are you with uncertainty avoidance?
- Do you like having policy and procedures to follow and feel happy with detailed guidance?

If yes:

- Do you expect service users to understand the requirements of organisational policies and procedures?
- How do you regard a service user who is challenging of the procedures that you are expected to follow?
- How do you respond to a colleague who appears to be constantly bending the rules?

If no:

- Do you get frustrated with what you see as petty bureaucracy?
- Do you feel restricted by the policies and guidelines that you have to follow? How do you behave if this is the case?
- How do you respond to a colleague who appears 'rule bound'?

What are the implications of both of these approaches for your organisation?

Consequences for organisations

In high uncertainty avoidance organisations there are expectations of greater attention to following the rules, so that risk can be minimised through detailed processes. The Social Work Reform Board (2010) has acknowledged that we have probably gone too far towards high uncertainty avoidance expectations, meaning that people are not confident about making decisions on an individual basis and are too bound up in following procedures and completing the necessary documentation. However, it will be some time before staff feel freed up to be creative and flexible in their approaches, having been required to pay close attention to the rules for so long.

Table 3.2 Comparison of low and high uncertainty avoidance

Low uncertainty avoidance	High uncertainty avoidance
Less structuring of activities	More structuring of activities
Fewer written rules	More written rules
More generalists or amateurs	Larger number of specialists
Organisations can be pluriform	Organisations should be as uniform as possible (standardisation)
Managers more involved in strategy	Managers more involved in details
Managers more interpersonal oriented and flexible in their style	Managers more task oriented and consistent in their style
Managers more willing to make individual and risky decisions	Managers less willing to make individual and risky decisions
High labour turnover	Lower labour turnover
More ambitious employees	Less ambitious employees
Lower satisfaction scores	Higher satisfaction scores
Less power through control of uncertainty	More power through control of uncertainty

From Hofstede (2001).

The extracts from the Munro report (2011a) have already shown how children's departments have become high uncertainty avoidance organisations; the final report clearly indicates that this is not compatible with high quality social work, and recommends ways of developing the organisation's ways of managing risk.

> The review's analysis of current problems identified that some of the constraints experienced by practitioners and their managers were attributed to statutory guidance and the inspection culture. Many complain that practice has become focused on compliance with guidance and performance management criteria, rather than on using these as a framework to guide the provision of effective help to children. The review has concluded that statutory guidance needs to be revised and the inspection process modified so that they enable and encourage professionals to keep a clearer focus on children's needs and to exercise their judgment on how to provide services to children and families. (Munro 2011b, Chapter 3, p.39)

A change in uncertainty avoidance will come as a relief to some workers, particularly those recruited a long time ago when the whole national culture was low uncertainty avoidance and who have found the recent high uncertainty avoidance approach very constraining. However, more-recently recruited social workers may well find it difficult to adapt to a less risk averse environment and may feel threatened by it. There will need to be a great deal of support for all concerned as organisations work to change this aspect of their culture.

High masculinity (vs. femininity)

This lens explores the quality of life issues and relates to cultural differences around the demonstration of emotions. It is about masculinity and femininity as concepts around behaviours, rather than biological differences. Hofstede (2001, Chapter 6) describes the predominant socialising pattern in most cultures as expecting men to be more assertive and women to be more nurturing, but that these expectations vary between societies. In high masculinity cultures emotions are to be controlled and not expressed. The culture endorses assertiveness, competition and aggressive success. Attention is given to material comfort, social privilege, status and prestige and ability to consume, and there is a belief that any individual who wants these can have them. If people don't achieve these it is because they have not worked hard enough, or they do not have the ability or character to achieve them, so do not deserve them. These cultural characteristics were certainly evident in children's literature in the UK in the past. The influence of a high masculinity culture led to greater differentiation of gender roles in children's books, with fathers typically being depicted as going out to work while mothers stayed at home and undertook domestic tasks. The boys went out and had adventures and the girls stayed at home and helped mother. Even today, children's advertising tends to show little girls playing quietly and cooperatively with each other, whilst little boys are more likely to be shown climbing, achieving feats of strength or speed and rushing around with action toys.

Case study

One half term when I had no support for the week, I felt I had to force the issue by 'doing a bunk' while my son was out with care workers. I rang the social workers to say I would not be at home when they returned him. The messages left for me were threatening, horrible – you must come back. It was awful. My son went to a children's home some distance away. No one came to see me while my son was away to talk about why I had taken such action. (Parent of disabled child)

- How does this example suggest that the social worker is high masculinity?

- What do you think the effects were on the service user of their experience of this approach?

Low masculinity cultures believe that emotions should be open and shared, valued and recognised. Value is placed on modesty, compromise and cooperative success. Cultures with these beliefs accept that some people do not have the ability, character or opportunity to achieve social success, as often these are accidents of birth. Socialisation is the process by which individual learn their role in society and the attendant expected behaviours.

In recent years in Europe women have taken on far more of a high masculinity culture. The feminist movement emphasised that women could achieve as much as men and did not have to be constrained by their gender or their biological clock. The communication style in a high masculinity culture will be more assertive and competitive yet Lakoff (1975) found that women still engaged in less masculinity language in their interactions, being more likely to apologise ('I'm not sure if this is a good idea but...', 'I may be wrong, but...', 'You may think this silly...', 'You may not like what I am going to say, but...'), more likely to take the blame if there is any misunderstanding, more likely to check out the other person's thoughts and feelings, and less likely to impose their own approach. Tannen (2001) found that even in less overtly high masculinity countries, such as the UK and USA, men still talked for longer in meetings; at conferences women presented 40 per cent of papers, made up 42 per cent of audiences yet only asked 27 per cent of questions.

Points to consider

In your next team meeting or training event, take notice of:

- who speaks first (male or female)

- who speaks for longest

- who interrupts others

- who has the last word.

What do you make of this?

What does this mean for the masculinity–femininity continuum in social care?

As Western cultures have become more egalitarian and it has become acceptable for women to display high masculinity characteristics and men to demonstrate lower masculinity preferences, there has been a degree of impatience, intolerance and incomprehension at women who appear to succumb to the more traditional behaviours. The wearing of a hijab or burkha, the preference to remain as a traditional 'housewife', a willingness to walk several paces behind a husband and not accept non-family visitors without him being present, can all attract a critical reaction, even from women workers who know it is irrational, but whose response is influenced by their awareness of their own journey and contributions towards a less high masculinity society.

On the other hand there is also intolerance of women who have embraced a more high masculinity style, with women who are assertive and seek to compete on an equal playing field with men being seen in a derogatory light. Indeed if a woman and a man both exhibit the same assertive behaviours, the woman is likely to be perceived as more aggressive than the man. These women often attract a range of language which would not be used about men who display similar behaviours. Masculinity is still a contested approach in many societies and constantly open to renegotiation, between the sexes, between different subcultural groups and between different generations.

Case study

Trudi was born in Germany, and 18 months ago she came to the UK to work in an adult services team. The agency has been going through a difficult time, with staff shortages, an impending reorganisation, and everyone feeling stressed and overwhelmed by high workloads and constant demands. There is often pressure to take on more cases, and many workers in the team feel unable to refuse, even though they already have more than they can manage. Trudi has consistently resisted taking on any of this new work, and has been very assertive in saying 'no' when asked; she now has the lowest caseload of anyone in the team, although still more than is recommended by the workload management policy. Trudi is also very vocal in team meetings, often openly challenging the managers, but she rarely joins in the informal discussions between colleagues. She is beginning to be seen as unsympathetic and self-centred by her colleagues, definitely not a 'team' player. For her part, Trudi doesn't quite understand why there seems to be a 'cooling off' of relationships between herself and her colleagues.

- How might a difference in high masculinity dimensions contribute to this difference of approach?

- How might an understanding of high masculinity contribute to a discussion about how the cultures differ and how this is being experienced?

- How might you approach a discussion with Trudi about high masculinity and what is going on?

Countries with high masculinity cultures can demonstrate these in very different ways. In Italy the explicit use of women as 'accessories', television programmes and the political situation all demonstrate that it is a very high masculinity world. In Japan it is evident in a very different way because the competitiveness and assertiveness are masked by the very formal patterns of communication. Scandinavian countries tend to be the lowest; childcare facilities are taken seriously, paternal rights are strongly valued and women hold many of the high posts in politics and business. Their pedagogical approach to children who commit offences probably gives a good indicator of a society which values nurture, understanding and personal development over retribution, punishment and individual blame/responsibility.

Points to consider

- Where do you sit on the masculinity–femininity continuum?

- Do you respond positively to an assertive and emotionally controlled environment?

If yes:

- How do you respond to emotional responses from service users?

- What do you think about people expressing their opinions openly and forcefully?

- How assertive do you think it is appropriate to be with colleagues and service users?

- What indicators of respect do you expect from colleagues in other organisations?

If no:

- Do you get concerned if service users are not able to express their feelings?

- Do you feel uncomfortable if a service user is being very assertive and challenging?

- How do you work with a colleague who you experience as very assertive and ambitious?

- How safe is it for you to express concern about others and engage in nurturing behaviours?

Consequences for organisations

At the time of Hofstede's research the UK was relatively high masculinity. Table 3.3 suggests that the current situation is more ambiguous and that for some of these indicators social care organisations are lower, particularly in regards to women achieving higher status roles within directorates but others aspects remain relatively high. However, gender considerations are less at the forefront of discussion and attention than they used to be.

Table 3.3 Comparison of low and high masculinity organisations

Low masculinity	High masculinity
Some young men and women want careers, others do not	Young men expect to make a career; those who don't, see themselves as failures
Organisations should not interfere with people's private lives	Organisational interests are a legitimate reason for interfering with people's private lives
More women in more qualified and better paid jobs	Fewer women in more qualified and better paid jobs
Women in more qualified jobs not particularly assertive	Women in more qualified jobs are very assertive
Lower job stress and less industrial conflict	Higher job stress and more industrial conflict
Appeal of job restructuring permitting group integration	Appeal of job restructuring permitting individual achievement

From Hofstede (2001).

High individualism vs. collectivism

This lens describes how much each individual sees that they hold responsibility for themselves or to what degree there is a collective approach, so behaviours are prescribed by others. A lot of social work practice in the UK is about encouraging service user independence and autonomy, yet for some cultures this would not be a desirable outcome.

High individualism means each person looks after themselves, with a focus on self-sufficiency, and other people may be seen to be competitors. People operate primarily as individuals, and expect other people to do the same.

Low individualist cultures are composed of tight communities where people operate as members of a group, and expect to look after others of their group and in turn to be looked after. The definition of 'group' becomes extremely important: who is included and who is not. In low individualist organisations the personal relationship often prevails over the task. Members of the group look to others in the group to look after them in times of need. Perhaps the most well-known low individualist group are the Amish of Lancaster County in America who reject individualism, including self-promotion. As a group they embrace an 'all being equal' approach, self-sufficiency and cooperation between members of the group. Humility and conforming to group norms is valued, no individual member of the group would seek to be seen as superior to or different from the others.

It is interesting in terms of motivational theory, based on American and European norms, that Maslow (1954) puts self-efficacy at the top of the pyramid in his hierarchy of needs, but people from collectivist cultures would not see that as the pinnacle of achievement, as the success of the group is much more important than individual achievement. In high individualist cultures self-praise and, indeed, arrogance are commonplace and accepted, whilst in low cultures these are disapproved of. In terms of influence on organisational behaviour this is possibly the most important of Hofstede's lenses.

Case study

When mentoring a very experienced and effective social worker through a post-qualifying award, the mentor noticed the social worker appeared to become slightly uncomfortable when talking about her talents and achievements, and was inclined to 'play down' her successes. In exploring this with her, the social worker explained that she had been brought up in a small town in Norway by middle-aged parents with a middle-class approach to child rearing. 'Although they were keen for me to do well and to succeed academically, to them and the society we lived in "beskjedenhet" was the most important quality to possess.' The dictionary translation of 'beskjeden' is 'unassuming', or 'modest'. '"Beskjeden" is not about *not* having confidence in yourself or doubting your own worth, but somehow about showing respect to others for who they are and not believing you are better than they are just because you do not share a common value system.'

(Norway is medium low in individualism but also low in power distance, giving rise to this restrained approach to self-aggrandisement.)

How conflict is managed differs between these two cultures. In high individualist cultures conflict is dealt with directly through competition and problem solving. A high individualist culture will encourage everybody to say openly what is on their mind and express their own needs and rights, even if it is hurtful to others around them. Low individualist cultures will seek to resolve conflict in more indirect ways that attempt to preserve the relationships. More effort is made to develop team working and more time is spent on communication and negotiation and there is more interest in harmony-enhancing conflict resolution techniques, such as mediation.

Individualism influences expectations, commitment and behavioural decision making patterns. High individualist people wish to avoid being submissive to authority figures and prefer to do things their own way. Lower individualist people find it easier to take advice and respond to cues from coworkers about how best to achieve a harmonious working environment.

In a high individualist culture children will be socialised to be responsible for their own needs; get their own meals, dress themselves from an early age, take care of themselves, and not make demands on others. The family won't involve people from extended family or the neighbours. Self-sufficiency is all important. Such a family wouldn't want to be involved with family mediation conferencing, and indeed might wish to keep any sort of assistance away, as the focus is on coping. Indeed they might believe that child protection services are an infringement of their human rights because they are interfering with their personal business.

Case study

Maurice, a black social work student originally from Ghana, was struggling during his second practice placement. His first placement had been undemanding, but he now found himself in a children's team undertaking initial assessments and often working with families in crisis.

His work base supervisor was concerned that sometimes during the beginning of an interview Maurice came across to family members as vague and a little disinterested; it seemed to take him a long time to 'get to the point'. She also felt he was also too accepting of what parents told him on occasions, and did not seem able to challenge them when necessary. She wondered if this was an indication that he lacked assertiveness and the ability critically to analyse the situation.

In talking to Maurice about her concerns he agreed that he found it difficult to challenge parents. In his country dignity and a good reputation is important; people try to maintain harmony during discussions to avoid causing anyone discomfort or embarrassment. Also, there are key differences in communication style between the two cultures – Ghanaians are more indirect communicators and will often convey messages in a more roundabout way, taking care not to cause offence. Added to this, in Ghana older people are considered wise and have higher status in the family, and it is usually accepted that they will make decisions according to what they perceive to be in the best interests of the family.

(Very few African countries were included in Hofstede's original analysis, but these behaviours would suggest that cultural expectations were low individualism and high power distance.)

On the other extreme, in a very low individualist culture it can appear that there is not an understanding of 'I'. Everything will be in terms of 'We'.

Points to consider

- Where do you see yourself on the individualism–collectivism continuum?
- Do you see yourself as an operator who just happens to have to fit in an organisational environment?

If yes:

- How do you maintain your individuality?

- What do you do if colleagues are trying to engage you in collective responsibilities?

- How do you respond to service users who appear very deferential to their family?

- What indicators of respect do you expect from colleagues in other organisations?

If no:

- Do you wish that teamwork was more active, encouraging of coworking, important and included social activities? If so, what could you do to facilitate this?

- What do you feel is important about establishing a collaborative approach in working with service users and how might you achieve it in your own practice and within your team?

- How differently do you experience multi-disciplinary working where a collective approach can be more difficult to create?

Consequences for organisations

Since individualism–collectivism is about how people relate to each other, it is, in some respects, the most important dimension within organisations. In a high individualism organisation people will say things without worrying about the impact that this is having on the receiver. They may feel free to say what is on their mind and be 'indifferent to the effect of what they say on the hearer's face' (Guirdham 2005, p.100). Within a social work organisation this is obviously the antipathy of what the organisation stands for, yet there may be little conscious attention given to enhancing collectivism. However, there is also little attention to dealing with service users who are high individualist, so if the culture is more collectivist, some workers may struggle to deal with overt expressions of self-interest. This dimension offers an interesting dilemma for organisations about how they wish to position themselves. Individualism encourages people to take responsibility for themselves, to avoid having to be submissive to those in authority and collectivism works hard to achieve harmonious working relationship.

Table 3.4 Comparison of low and high individualism

Low individualism	High individualism
Involvement of individuals with organisations primarily moral	Involvement of individual with organisations primarily calculative
Employees expect organisations to look after them like a family – and can become very alienated if organisation dissatisfies them	Organisations are not expected to look after employees from cradle to the grave
Organisation has great influence on members' wellbeing	Organisation has moderate influence on members' wellbeing
Employees expect organisation to defend their interest	Employees are expected to defend their own interests
Policies and practices based on loyalty and sense of duty	Policies and practice should allow for individual initiative
Promotion from inside local focus	Promotion from inside and outside cosmopolitan focus
Promotion on seniority	Promotion on market value
Less concern with fashion in management ideas	Managers try to be up to date and endorse modern management ideas
Policies and practices vary according to relations (particularism)	Policies and practices apply to all (universalism)

From Hofstede (2001).

Conclusion

This chapter has explored a particular model of understanding diversity, developed from researching national cultures but equally applicable to organisational cultures. It highlights how people may be judged when they are operating in different places on these dimensions and how this may affect how workers interact with them. Social workers need to be alert to both their own and their service users' cultural norms. Each may have problems with differing cultural expectations and struggle with understanding the other. Greater overt discussion about cultural norms and diversity may be very beneficial to the working relationship.

Issues from this chapter to discuss with your supervisor

1. Where you think you are on each of the dimensions.

2. Where you think your organisation is on each of the dimensions.

3. How well you fit with the organisational culture.

4. How you may need to adapt to cope the organisational culture.

5. How changes in organisational culture will impact on how you work.

Further reading and resources

Harrison, R., Harvey, R. and Maclean, S. (2010) *Developing Cultural Competence in Social and Health Care*. Staffordshire: Kirwin Maclean Associates Ltd.

Hofstede, G. www.geerthofstede.nl/geert.aspx – for Hofstede's own website.

Hofstede, G. www.geert-hofstede.com/hofstede_dimensions.php – for a summary of the positions of different countries on the four dimensions.

Reder, P., Duncan, S. and Gray, M. (1993) *Beyond Blame: Child Abuse Tragedies Revisited*. London: Routledge.

Tannen, D. (1989) *That's Not What I Meant*. London: Virago.

Tannen, D. (1995) *Talking From 9 to 5: Women and Men at Work*. London: Virago.

Tannen, D. (2001) *You Just Don't Understand: Men and Women in Conversation*. London: Virago.

Tseung, W. and Hsu, J. (1979) 'Culture and psychotherapy.' In A.J. Marsella, R. Thorp and T. Giborowski (eds) *Perspectives on Cross-Cultural Psychology*. New York, NY: Academic Press.

Vaughan, M. (1977) 'Overseas students: some cultural clues.' *UKCOSA News 9*, 1, Spring/Summer.

CHAPTER 4

Learning Styles

Key messages

- Theories about how people learn.
- We need to know and understand our own learning styles and personal preferences.
- We can then identify other people's styles and preferences.
- We can adapt our style and interactions to work with other's strengths and develop their less preferred styles.

Introduction

One of the important aspects of working with service users and colleagues is to understand how they learn, particularly if we are having a long-term involvement with them. Most of our work takes place with people who need to develop their life skills and to learn new ways of operating. Parents need to develop their childcare skills, knowledge about stages of child development and how to change their responses to be appropriate for the level of the child's development. Older people need to learn how to manage their environment as their mobility and manual dexterity decrease, and to adapt to life which may have a very different pattern to previous experiences, for example, retirement after a lifetime of work. Young people need to develop their consequential thinking skills, so that they can anticipate the outcomes of their actions. As practitioners we are also learning all of the time and need to be sensitive to how we ourselves learn and how our colleagues may be learning in a completely different way. Style of learning is one of the many ways in which we differ, so it is an important consideration in thinking about diversity.

Learning cycles

As pressure increases for reflective practice (Munro 2011a and SWRB 2010) one of the models that has established itself as the basis for this (Morrison 2010) is the work of Kolb, who developed the concept of the learning cycle based observation of how people absorb information. Many social workers complete a learning styles questionnaire as part of their training but thereafter have it as passive knowledge, rather than actively using the cycle to ensure that their own practice learns from all parts of the cycle, and to be alert to service users' preferences, in order to match their interaction to those preferences.

The Kolb model (1984) is not about intelligence level or an individual's cognitive ability, but how each person best makes sense of new experiences and learning. Kolb suggests that in order to learn completely we need to go through a four-stage process.

The stages are:

1. Concrete experience – to experience actively something on a day-to-day basis.

2. Reflective observation – to reflect on it to begin to draw out learning.

3. Abstract conceptualisation – to see how the experience fits with our previous learning and understanding of the world.

4. Active experimentation – to see if the new learning really works again, in practice.

This can be depicted as follows:

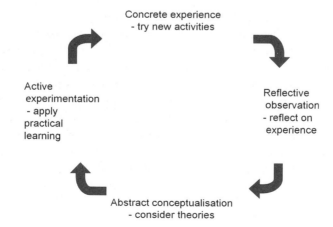

Figure 4.1 Kolb's Learning Cycle

It is suggested that to order to learn people have to keep going around the cycle. Watching a child play, this cycle can often be seen in action. Children can be observed playing, then they will sit down and think or talk about what they have been doing. They then frequently ask questions and try to fit the activity into their model of the world, as they currently understand it, before having another go, to see if it will really work again.

However, just as some children can more easily be observed going through all four stages than others, so as adults some of us are more skilled at going through all four stages.

An example of this learning cycle in practice:

Case study

Mary, a new worker, was asked to watch while her colleague used a hoist to lift Joe, a child aged 10, who has severe physical disabilities. At the time she simply did as she was asked and stood out of the way and observed what happened (**Concrete Experience**).

When Mary thought about it afterwards, she wondered what Joe thought about her being there, and realised she hadn't spoken to him at all. She also realised she wasn't really sure what her role had been (**Reflection observation**).

Mary decided to go and look at the moving and handling policy for the agency and when she read it she saw that a second person was there to assist with the hoist and offer additional support. She went on to look at the Charter of Children's Rights in the agency, and thought about the part that said children have a right to choices, to be treated with respect and to be kept safe (**Abstract conceptualisation**).

Mary decided that next time she was asked to help with moving and hoisting she would go and talk to the child first, and make sure he knew who she was and was happy to have her help; also that she would agree with the other worker what each of them would do during the move, and make sure that they talked to the child at each stage to reassure him he was safe (**Active experimentation**).

Table 4.1 Exercise

Using Kolb's model think of an incident from your professional life (it can be something quite simple) and complete each box in Table 4.1.

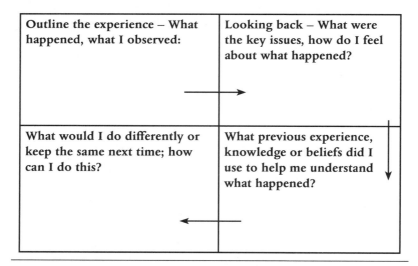

Outline the experience – What happened, what I observed:	Looking back – What were the key issues, how do I feel about what happened?
What would I do differently or keep the same next time; how can I do this?	What previous experience, knowledge or beliefs did I use to help me understand what happened?

Questionnaires

Honey and Mumford (1982, 1983, 2006) have developed the idea of learning styles from the work of Kolb and suggest that all of us have preferences for how we learn. There is a version of their questionnaire available online at www.peterhoney.com. This offers the opportunity for each person to discover their own learning style preferences. The questionnaire tends to show that most people have a preference for learning in one or two of the styles and will learn more confidently and effectively through those than some of the others. The preferences are added to the diagram in Figure 4.2.

The learning styles questionnaire they developed allows each person to explore their learning preferences at the point in time at which they complete it. These preferences can change over time, depending on circumstances and the requirements of what is going on in an individual's life, such as a change of role or job, so it is important that the preferences are not seen as fixed and irreversible.

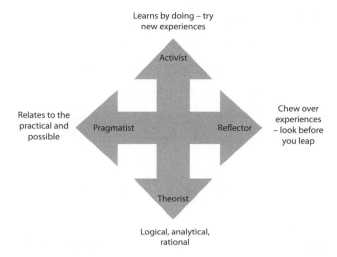

Figure 4.2 Learning styles preferences

Case study

When Ellie began a part time post-qualifying course after six years of 'front line' social work she completed a learning styles questionnaire which showed her preferred learning style at the time to be 'activist'. Ten years later, having moved out of direct social work practice and spent five years as a practice teacher and assessor, she repeated the questionnaire and this time found her preferred learning style to be 'reflector'.

All of these questionnaires are only an indication of selected preferences, and may vary according to how honest a person is with themselves, how they feel at the time they fill them in, what job they are doing at any one time and possibly what they think the 'right' answers should be. Not that there are any 'right' answers!

Preferences linked to learning styles

In planning work with service users and colleagues it is helpful to be able to recognise the preferences linked to the different learning styles.

Activists learn best when

- there are new experiences to learn from
- they can engross themselves in 'here and now' activities
- there are a range of diverse activities
- they can generate ideas without constraints
- they are thrown in at the deep end
- they are involved with other people
- they can 'have a go'.

Case study

Ashok is a young care leaver who has been mixing with a crowd of young people who regularly cause trouble in the community. He has taken a couple of bikes and caused some minor damage to a shop, for which he's received a warning from the police. Ashok thinks what he did was just a bit of a laugh, but admits he was goaded into it by the others and did it because he didn't want to lose face with them. His social worker thinks if nothing changes it won't be long before he commits a serious criminal offence, and finds himself 'on a slippery slope'.

Ashok finds it difficult to sit still and is always looking for something to fiddle with; he is happiest when he's working on mechanical tasks, like stripping down and rebuilding his bike. His social worker found him a place on a local project building stock cars. Each session involves physical activity, building and testing the cars, alongside group work focusing on self-esteem, confidence building and managing impulsive behaviours. This proved to be ideal for Ashok; it has helped him think more about his actions and choices, while at the same time keeping him productively occupied in an activity he loves with others who shared his enthusiasms.

Reflectors learn best when

- they can observe/think over activities
- they can stand back from events
- they are allowed time to think and prepare

- they can research

- they can review

- they are asked to produce reports

- they can exchange views in a protected environment

- they can operate to their own deadlines.

Case study

Darren has a serious drug habit. He is trying to survive on methadone, and has engaged in long discussions with his social worker about the difference of the impact on him between illegal drugs, and his current prescription.

He is currently living in a hostel, and would like to get his own tenancy, but never quite gets around to going to the meeting with a housing worker who would help.

He is really enthused about the idea of spending time looking at what he would like to make of his life, and what impact his current behaviours are having on both him and his family.

He has expressed an interest in understanding more about how drugs work on the body, and what the process of detox might be like for him, with a view to developing the best and easiest strategy for weaning himself off methadone. He knows he needs to think about ways to overcome the barriers he sees at the moment.

The objectives in working with him for the next few months could well focus on these areas, and start to move him around the learning cycle converting some of his thoughts into action.

Theorists learn best when

- they are offered interesting theories

- there is time to explore ideas

- there is opportunity to question

- they are intellectually stretched

- there are structured situations with a clear purpose

- they can read about logical ideas/concepts

- they can analyse success or failure

- they can participate in complex situations.

Case study

Richard sexually abused his daughter and one of her friends. He attended the Sex Offenders Treatment Programme whilst in prison, and is living in a hostel until he finds somewhere permanent to live. He is attending a relapse prevention group. He asks lots of searching questions of the tutors, trying hard to make sure he understands what is being said. He is quick to spot any inconsistencies.

He is really interested in being able to see his daughter again and wishes to work hard to convince her social worker that he is a fit person.

He has absorbed many of the models and theories about sex offending and is inclined to question any new suggestions about behaviour, until he sees how these ideas fit with the concepts he now knows so well.

He is enthusiastic about the idea of one of his objectives being around working out for himself how any new knowledge will be 'bolted on' to his existing models, but is also interested in moving on to having some practical objectives about trying out his ideas and theories in his day-to-day life.

Pragmatists learn best when

- there are links between the topic and their job

- they can try things out and receive feedback

- they can emulate the model provided

- they are shown techniques which are applicable to their job

- they can implement what has been learned

- the learning activity has validity

- they can concentrate on practical issues.

Case study

Wayne has recently begun living with his new partner, Sue, and their baby son. In the past Wayne assaulted a previous girlfriend, and knows that if something like that ever happens in this relationship Sue will make him leave. He was offered anger management sessions previously, but said he couldn't see the point of them. He has never thought about issues around gender and power, and wasn't convinced that talking would make any difference to his own lifestyle.

The social worker has recognised there is now an opportunity of working with Wayne; he is more motivated than previously as he wants to stay with Sue and their son, and knows he will only have one chance at this. Wayne says he wants practical objectives which make immediate sense to him: 'If I do something, she will stay' and is willing to work to find out what that 'something' might be. He says that if he can see that it makes sense and works then he will give it a go.

Points to consider

Think of a recent positive example when you learned something new – a skill around a new area of practice, a piece of information or a different way of doing something.

- How did you learn it?

- What made it a positive learning experience?

- What does this tell you about how you usually learn new things?

Case study

Very recently on a training event for foster parents, a small group of participants had spent some time together over the coffee break and had collectively come to the conclusion that the material was being presented too slowly for them. After the break they expressed this view very vociferously, but then several other people who had not been part of that group expressed an opposite viewpoint, stating that the pace was just right for them. One of the participants later expressed surprise that anybody had seen the experience differently from the collective view of the small group. We all sometimes forget that everybody else's experience of the world is different from our own.

As indicated earlier, Honey and Mumford (2006) give very clear explanations of how people in each of the four styles prefer to learn. The relevance of these differences to the supervisory process is also covered in the *Mastering Social Work Supervision* (Wonnacott 2012) book in this series. Each stage in the process is essential and we all have to work on learning for ourselves. It is not something that can be done *to* us, nor *for* us, only *by* us. In a busy world it is very easy to get into a short circuit, whereby we do something, then do it again, sometimes just trying harder. It is the reflection stage that adds value to the actions, otherwise we can have years of experience and not learn anything from it.

What the authors have discovered, however, from the questionnaires that have been completed by the staff in the social care sector, is that they do not reflect the preferences of the population as a whole as researched by Honey and Mumford (1982, 1983). Without looking at other organisations and groups, practitioners are likely to assume that the learning style profile in their workplace is 'normal', and will be the same in the wider world. Completing the questionnaire with very large numbers of staff across four probation services, including every person in one service, came up with the following profile:

Reflectors: 55 per cent

Theorists: 25 per cent

Pragmatists: just above 10 per cent

Activists: just below 10 per cent

(Gast 2000, unpublished)

The author's recent experience suggests that this profile also appears to be consistent across social care teams. In these organisations the preferred style of learning would be to sit down, ideally in a small group, and have time to 'chew things over'. Traditionally the service user came in, sat in an office and was asked to reflect on her/his recent experiences, a preference which suited the workers well, but does not necessarily meet the learning preferences of the service user. In the wider world the preference is more strongly activist, learning through doing, hence the social care professions being seen as 'too much talking and not enough action'.

In order to work most effectively with service users, practitioners need to know their learning strengths and preferences. For example, some service users may find structured learning more difficult; they may have less formal experience of it and so their repertoire for learning in this way is less developed, or the experiences they have had of learning in this way may be negative. Group work experiences which set up a formal learning environment, be it for foster carers, parents or substance misusers, will militate against learning for those who did not flourish in the school setting. As practitioners we need to work more towards getting the environment right to harness the learning strengths of the service user, and carefully develop their other stages of learning. 'He started with the practical things. What we needed to get going. He then moved on to parenting classes, and then me talking about my ex-wife. That was exactly right for me' (refugee father talking about his social worker).

However, just because a person has a preference for one particular learning style, it does not mean that they cannot use the other learning styles successfully. Some people are very evenly balanced in terms of which is their strongest preference, and most practitioners have developed skills in using each of the styles and stages in learning, even if they are slightly less proficient at some.

Case study

I knew he didn't read and write very well, so I used a picture to get him to reflect on what children need. However, what I didn't take into account was his learning style. He was completely intimidated by sitting at a table with a paper task, even though I had provided a picture. He did have a lot of insight but it was only through practical activities that I was able to draw them out. (Student social worker engaging with a dyslexic and activist child)

Points to consider

- What do you know about your own learning style?
- How strong are your preferences?
- How do you work with your less strong learning styles?
- What do you know about the learning style of your supervisor/supervisees?
- How do you develop a sense of the learning styles of your service users?
- How do you talk about the differences or similarities between your styles?

- How are these differences taken into account in how you present materials to different people?

- How can you adapt materials that you might be using with different people to enhance their learning potential?

- On a training event how do you spot when the sessions have been designed to engage the different learning styles?

- How easy is it to use people's different learning styles as something to value, rather than a label to put on them and an excuse for not focusing on other styles?

Reflective practice

In terms of reflective practice social workers do, of course, need to go all the way around the cycle. 'Professional development occurs through the process of making use of and learning from experience, reflection on that experience, analysing it with reference to values, theory, research and thereby developing new models for action which are then tested through further experience' Morrison (2001, p.57). Because of personal preference or the pressurised working environment, workers tend not to do all the elements effectively, and it is easy for people to skim over their less preferred stages to reach a practical plan. This model has been taught to staff supervisors for several years, but each practitioner needs to embed its use into their day-to-day work. Serious case reviews (Reder *et al.* 1993) have demonstrated that it is all too easy to do the 'quick fix' from experience to action planning without enough attention to reflection and analysis.

Figure 4.3 Using the cycle to ensure safe practice

Visual, auditory, kinaesthetic (VAK) learning styles

Another way of classifying preferences for taking in information is the visual, auditory and kinaesthetic learning styles model. This is probably one of the easier means of noticing how people are learning and to apply in work with service users, and is used widely within the education system. However, the ease of application should not belie the importance of this approach, both to the learner, and to the effectiveness of communication.

Visual learners will take in information best through their eyes. In order to make sense of what is being communicated they will want to see it in some form. Many people have this preference, which is why so many lecturers, teachers, etc., use some sort of visual aid. For example, when a young service user needs to learn a new activity, such as basic childcare, it is far easier for a visual learner to understand what is required of them when there is a demonstration of necessary processes, than to hear just a verbal description of what to do. By visualising what is required the skills are more likely to become embedded. Visual people like to work out their ideas by writing them down or drawing them. They will often prefer to see something on paper to a discussion.

On the other hand, auditory learners would be more satisfied with a verbal description of what is required. They are tuned into making sense of the world through what they hear. They are likely to be more overtly articulate than others, and better able to describe out loud what is expected of them and what they are doing. They will rely more on hearing what is going on around them, and will be sensitive to extraneous noises, which they can find very distracting. They often need to work out their ideas by talking about them with others. When they say something out loud, it becomes real to them. Working with auditory service users may require the worker to be patient as the person 'thinks out aloud' and the most effective way of knowing how much an individual has taken in will be to ask them to describe their understanding.

Kinaesthetic learners will take information in through their physical senses, experiencing what it feels like. It is almost as though there is an imprint of the actual muscular activity in the brain, hence 'flying by the seat of your pants'. Again the person learning a physical activity will FEEL the movement, will be able to absorb what is required of the body, and will be able to reproduce that movement accurately. An example of this is when someone who hasn't ridden a bicycle for many years is then able to get on one and ride, albeit a bit wobbly at first! Kinaesthetic also refers to emotions because it seems that emotional feelings and bodily feelings are closely tied together in our brains, so kinaesthetic people will also learn from the emotions that are engendered by a learning experience. They will often learn best by trying out, doing and experiencing.

In fact, most people learn best when using a combination of preferences. The dominant mode of learning is then reinforced by the other two modes. For example, a visual person must have visual input but is helped by kinaesthetic and auditory experiences. However, a visual person attending a lecture will be disadvantaged where information is only given verbally, as will an auditory person faced only with a written paper. This is why so many presentations now involve both speaking and overheads on PowerPoint! Traditionally talk and chalk (auditory and visual) was the way of teaching, whereas writing (visual and kinaesthetic) is the way in which learners absorb information and express themselves.

In practice

To be an effective practitioner, workers need to try to develop communication techniques that combine all three styles: multi-sensory learning, using sight, sound and movement. In fact, most people learn from all three of these senses. To get the best out of communication, the preferred mode of the service user should be used, but it will need to be re-enforced by the other two.

People with these different preferences will use different language, and with practice workers are able to work out which preference others have from the words that they use.

People with a visual preference will say things such as:

- I see what you mean.

- I can picture that.

- That looks good to me.

- I like the look of that.

- I can't visualise that.

- I get the picture.

People with an auditory preference will say things such as:

- I hear what you say.

- That sounds alright to me.

- That doesn't sound right.

- Listen to me!

- It's music to my ears.

People with a kinaesthetic orientation will say things such as:

- That feels right to me.

- I get a sense of that.

- I can get a handle on that.

- Let's get to grips with things.

- I can figure it out.

All of these comments will be about UNDERSTANDING, not the actual physical experience involved. Using the wrong language may lose the other person, who may not be able to tune in to what you are trying to say, or see the point that you are making, or even get to grips with your argument!

Natural learning preferences are honed by life experience. Whatever our natural preferences, many of us have become increasingly conversant with receiving information visually through technology, to the extent where a new 'language' has evolved in the form of Textese or SMS (short message service). For the majority of young people, new technologies are an unquestioned part of their world, taken for granted as a source of learning. Some may have developed their visual experience through use of computer games requiring fast responses and focused concentration, but no requirement for them to engage in spoken dialogue. However, research into the possible consequences of this, if any, is sparse.

The Byron Review (2008) looked at the available research into the skills children learn through playing games and found it centres on visual attention, reaction times, the development of cognitive skills such as spatial perception or strategic thinking, planning or hypothesis testing (Durkin and Barber 2002). She also identified recent studies that have shown some improvements in decision making and attention in children of six years of age following training on a computer screen (Rueda *et al.* 2005).

There is currently speculation that video gaming could be used to enhance skills of flexibility (ability to shift from one task to another) and behavioural inhibition (ability to prevent oneself from doing something inappropriate) in children (Goswami 2008) and, as Byron (2008, p.155) comments: 'This would have a significant impact on their ability to regulate their own thoughts and behaviour, which is one of the developmental challenges of childhood and could be of great benefit to children.' However, she points out that research has not yet been undertaken to discover whether cognitive skills such as these can be improved significantly by such practice, or whether skills learned through a video game might be transferable to other 'real-life' situations. These are all areas that would benefit from further exploration, to establish what applications there might be for learning and development in both children and adults.

Experience of working with other groups of people who may experience difficulty in communication and learning may also help us. Many research studies have shown (e.g. Goleman 1996; Gross 2008) that autistic people struggle to make sense of the subtle elements of the facial expressions of others, failing to make sense of the emotions underpinning the kinaesthetic nature of facial movements. Communication with them therefore needs to be more direct and explicit. However, they tend to be visual learners; they understand what they see better than what they hear, and therefore visual strategies that support verbal communication are often very helpful. Using pictures, symbols, signs, photographs and objects of reference can all augment verbal communication. Not only might these be easier to understand, but there is the added advantage that their behaviour is predictable and so less likely to raise anxiety and detract from the message being conveyed; people can be experienced as unpredictable and anxiety provoking, whilst objects are more consistent and reliable. For many children who are able to use speech but find it difficult, combining verbal communication with signing can be helpful; augmenting the verbal communication with signing or pictures lessens the pressure on them to be fluent verbally.

Using videos has also been found helpful in enabling children and adults with learning difficulties to learn. Research studies with autistic young people, for instance, have found that videos can be used successfully to demonstrate positive behaviour, encourage social skills and teach a range of tasks. When using a recording of 'how to' undertake a specific task, young people learned to do the task correctly by imitating the behaviour they had seen in the video. In another example, a parent recorded a 'walk through' of what her son would need to do when he got to his new school: opening his locker, moving from hall to classroom, and from class to class. This helped him to prepare in advance for the first day. As well as tapping in to the autistic person's learning strength, because it is visual, a video recording has the advantage of being repeatable; the child or adult can watch it again and again, if possible controlling it themselves, which reduces their anxiety and aids learning.

Although the above examples involve learning in disabled children and young people, we do not mean to imply that they should be reserved for any one particular service user group; far from it. Working to the person's learning preferences, developing a range of techniques and using a combination or variety of approaches will promote communication and learning for all those we work with. Practitioners who are unlikely to have time to assess preferences through filling in learning styles questionnaires may benefit particularly from the identification of these differences in learning, as it is possible to distinguish these styles fairly quickly, by simply asking a few questions.

For visual clues

'Can you see what I am doing?'

'Does this look right to you?'

'Can you see how this works?'

'Does it help to watch what I am doing?'

People with a visual preference often tend to have a more upright posture, and dress neatly and carefully. They can be quick and sharp thinkers, but may say little. They will plan and remember by pictures, so directions via conspicuous landmarks will help. They may have difficulty remembering long verbal inputs, so may ask you to repeat things.

For auditory clues

'Can you hear how it works?'

'Does that sound alright to you?'

'Can you follow my instructions?'

'Does that sound sensible?'

People with an auditory preference will sometimes show less care about their looks or dress than others. They like to work out their ideas through discussion, so will talk a lot. However, there may be hesitations or pauses in the conversation, whilst they speak through an idea in their mind. When speaking they may be very fluent, articulate and persuasive. They will have a good memory for anything that you have said to them, but will not so easily remember written instructions. Encouraging auditory people to repeat things back to you is an excellent way of reinforcing learning.

For kinaesthetic clues

'Can you follow me?'

'Does that feel right to you?'

'How do you get a sense of that?'

'Can you get to grips with this?'

People with a kinaesthetic preference are more likely to dress in a warm, relaxed and cuddly way! They dress comfortably. They may well flop around, and are more likely to curl up than sit up. They learn from the feel of things and by experiencing them, so will learn best by having a go, rather than either written or verbal instructions.

Listening to the response, either confirming the preference through a repetition of the language, or moving to a different mode, will give lots of clues about how you can best demonstrate any techniques you are wanting service users to learn.

Case study

The visual, auditory and kinaesthetic learning styles do appear to be more culturally influenced than the Kolb styles.

A teacher who was interested in these cultural differences tried an experiment. She told a story to her class in England, then asked them to repeat it back to her. They could tell her the outline of the story and could draw some vivid pictures about the story.

Whilst spending some time with the school's 'twin' in Kenya, she told children of the same age the same story. They could repeat it back to her word for word, after only one telling, even though the subject matter was further from their life experience than it was for the English children, but they had difficulty with trying to draw pictures.

European culture is currently very visually oriented, with television, computers and billboard advertising being a day-to-day experience. In Kenya, the emphasis is still on the oral tradition, where stories are passed between generations by word of mouth and in many places access to books and pictures is still limited.

Understanding people's learning preferences may be of particular value when working with disabled people, particularly those who have a sensory or communication impairment. It is not simply about technique; the starting point needs to be an understanding of the impact of barriers such as societal discrimination and the power relations between professionals and disabled people. The unfair and unequal treatment of disabled people is built into organisations, their policies and practices at a structural level, as well as played out in the language, communication and professional–disabled service user interactions. Simply improving professionals' communication skills and developing a wider repertoire of tools for use with service users, although important, is not enough.

Disabled people, particularly those with learning disabilities, may find it difficult to make sense of information that is aimed at a general audience:

- They may have had different life experiences, and may not have experienced situations others may take for granted.

- They may also have had more negative experiences, such as being treated differently from others, meeting with intolerance from others, or being harassed.

- They may have had fewer opportunities to learn new skills, such as learning to drive, for instance.

Disabled people and their carers from black and ethnic minority groups may particularly have different experiences, lifestyles and ways of thinking, which may include how they access, make sense of and use information:

- They may have experienced discrimination on the grounds of race as well as disability, and this may have impacted particularly on their access to information and learning opportunities. For instance, they may have had limited access to libraries, evening classes, community centres or other places where people can get information and learn new skills.

- There may be generational differences, including the type of education they have had and how this impacts on their ability to learn in different ways.

- Some people may prefer to use their first language when communicating about sensitive topics or learning new skills.

- Some may not read and write fluently in any language.

- Different cultures prefer different ways of getting information and some tend to think some sources more reliable than others. For example, people from South Asian cultures often like to get information from people they know, who understand about the topic. They might not be happy with written information; they may feel unsure that the person who wrote it explained everything about the topic.

(Namaganda 2004)

It is not simply about having information translated, although this is good practice, it is important to know and understand the person's culture, religion, beliefs and values, their personal 'story of the world' and how these factors may impact on the way they prefer to communicate and learn. For example, it is often helpful to use pictures and photographs to augment communication with learning disabled people; however, the way people understand and use information and pictures varies from one culture to another. It is important to use only those images that are familiar to the person being communicated with, in terms of who is shown in the picture, their style of dress, facial expression, body language, what they are doing and the environment around them, for instance.

For people who have learning difficulties using step-by-step pictures showing how to undertake a task, role play, modelling, and videoing can all be helpful when learning new tasks. For some adopting a multi-sensory approach will be the most effective. Transferring learning and newly acquired skills from one setting to another can sometimes be difficult, so if possible work with the person where they will be using the skill. Repeating the learning event and opportunities for frequent practice are also often helpful.

Several organisations have produced guidelines and suggestions about how to present information in a helpful way when working with people with learning disabilities. Some general suggestions are:

- Decide what you want to say before you begin to say it. Break information down into small chunks and say it in a logical order.

- Keep sentences short. Just one idea or topic in each sentence is ideal. Ensure the person has understood before moving on.

- Think about the words and language you use. Keep it simple, clear and concise and use words you would use in everyday discussion rather than longer more complicated ones. Avoid using jargon, technical terms, acronyms and abbreviations. Use active verbs as much as possible, for instance say 'I will send it' rather than 'it will be sent by me'.

- Be accurate and precise – words like 'some', 'many', 'soon', and 'lots' will mean different things to different people.

- Be consistent and repeat words rather than using different words for the same thing. For instance, if you use the word 'smacking' in one sentence, don't use 'corporal punishment' or 'physical chastisement' in the next. Repeating words and phrases has the added advantage of helping people to remember the information.

- Use positive sentences wherever you can, as negatives can be harder to understand. For instance, 'you can come to the centre on Mondays and Wednesdays', rather than 'don't come to the centre on Tuesdays and Thursdays'.

- Make it interesting and relevant to the person you're communicating with. Use real life and examples that have meaning to them and their life where you can.

Case studies

The following comments from learning disabled service users illustrate the difference it made for them when their social worker considered how to communicate in ways that made sense to them:

She really made an effort, made the reports and stuff understandable to me (para 7.2, p.40).

She worked on what we could do, not what we couldn't do (para 7.2, p.39).

The social worker who came to the family group conference was great. She had prepared information to share with me and my family. She had it written on large pieces of paper and with not too many words. We all understood it. She had also asked me what I wanted to say, and we had put something together, and she said, you go first (para 7.4, p.40).

(Wiffin 2010)

Case study

Diego was allocated a case of a 16-month-old girl who had been removed from her mother, Julie, due to concerns about emotional neglect. When talking to Julie, Diego realised that she found it hard to understand the concerns that had been raised, and that Julie had felt intimidated by some of the previous discussions she had had with professionals. It was apparent Julie had limited ability to take on new information and quickly became confused, particularly when a lot of information was given to her verbally all at once.

Diego and Julie agreed to meet again to discuss the concerns, and Diego made some suggestions about how they might go about this. Julie chose the option of using a laptop as she was used to using a computer at home.

Before their next meeting Diego prepared a presentation on his laptop using images he scanned in from a book on child development. He began with a child's physical needs, then moved on to their emotional development and needs. He included pictures and animations, and left gaps for information to be added. The following week Diego took the presentation with him to Julie's and used it as a structure for their discussion. He began by checking out Julie's understanding of a child's physical needs, for example, asking her to identify these and then adding them in. He then went on to emotional needs, asking Julie to identify what all children need, and then supply information specific to her daughter so that they could add this in together.

Using this method Diego was able to assess Julie's level of knowledge and understanding of children's needs, and the potential impact of these not being met for her daughter. It also enabled him to broach difficult and sensitive topics in a non-confrontational and non-judgmental way, and involve Julie fully in the process.

At the end of the presentation Diego suggested he send Julie a printed version of the presentation they had completed together, as well as emailing a copy to her. They could then use these to plan their next session.

Correlation between the different models

There does not appear to be any direct correlation between these two models. It is possible that an activist may be more likely also to be kinaesthetic, that reflectors may be more inclined to be auditory and that theorists may be visual, but no research appears to have been undertaken to explore these issues. In discussing these different learning styles in training events in England and Wales, it seems that most social care staff recognise the Kolb/Honey and Mumford styles in themselves, their colleagues and their supervisees, and can start to apply them to their service users. People can also recognise that they have preferences, but the balance between the learning styles can change over time. For example, becoming more involved with developing others, such as taking on the role as a practice educator, can shift the balance towards developing a more theorist approach. With practice, social care staff become alert to the clues that service users offer, and can adapt their communications appropriately.

The visual, auditory and kinaesthetic approach can then be used as a method of ensuring successful communication, through actively using all three preferences which allows for the repetition of messages through a variety of approaches.

Many service users have had poor learning experiences, in their families and at school, and will protect themselves from what they might believe could be other potentially damaging experiences. It is therefore important to try to work with their strengths, use as many different approaches as possible to reinforce communication and resist any temptation to be impatient when someone is learning in a manner which is very different from one's own.

What situations make it easier for us to learn?

The educator Edgar Dale (1969) developed what became known as Dale's Cone of Learning, a rather complicated name for what is actually a simple idea that can be helpful when planning work with learners.

Dale looked at a range of learning opportunities to see how effective they were in terms of people being able to remember what they learned. He suggests that the nearer the learning experience was to real life and the more sensory channels participants used during the learning activity, the more likely they were to remember the learning. So if they used sight, hearing, touching and movement senses, for example by taking part in a live demonstration, they were more likely to learn from the event. If all they used was their sense of hearing, because someone was simply talking to them, they were less likely to remember and learn.

Other people have added percentages to Dale's cone, which is very controversial, but usually represented as:

People generally remember:

- 10 per cent of what they read

- 20 per cent of what they hear

- 30 per cent of what they see

- 50 per cent of what they hear and see

- 70 per cent of what they say or write.

Even if the percentages are open to question, the principles of learning still apply and reinforce the need to be open, creative and flexible in order to maximise learning for a diverse range of service users.

Table 4.2 Exercise: Assumptions around learning

This exercise will help you begin to identify your own assumptions about learners in general, and can be adapted to help you think about people and how they learn.

In the first column write down eight assumptions you tend to make about learners.

In the middle column identify the possible implications.

Use the third column to identify how you might accommodate different learners.

The example given relates to group work, but your assumptions should also include work with individual service users.

Assumption	Possible implication	What might you do to accommodate different learners
e.g. People find it easier to learn in groups if everyone is given information sheets to work through.	Someone who has difficulty with taking in written information might find this oppressive, but may not feel able to tell me this, particularly if in a group situation.	If possible find out in advance if anyone in the group has literacy or language differences. Ask one person in each group to volunteer to read out the questions and record the answers for the whole group.

Conclusion

This chapter has identified some models about how people learn and the impact of these on practice. Workers do need to know and actively engage with their own learning preferences in order to be aware of the impact that they might be having on others. The starting point for any interaction with a service user then needs to be an analysis of how they are going to best make sense of the intervention. The worker should reflect on both their own and their service user's learning preferences; similarities, differences, areas for potential misunderstanding or miscommunication, as the foundation for effective engagement.

Issues from this chapter to discuss with your supervisor

1. Identify your learning preferences and those of your supervisor.

    ✓ What are the implications of any similarities and differences for the way that you work together?

    ✓ What strengths and weaknesses might these preferences have on your interactions with service users?

    ✓ What areas might you need to concentrate on to develop your practice?

    ✓ What signs and signals do you need to be alert to from service users that might indicate you are not harnessing their best learning abilities?

Further reading and resources

CHANGE www.changepeople.co.uk. Includes a downloadable guide: *How to Make Information Accessible: A Guide to Producing Easy Read Documents.*

The Children's Society (2008) *My life, My Decisions, My Choice: Involving Disabled Children and Young People in the Decision-making Process.* London: The Children's Society. Guidance notes for professionals. See also their Disability Toolkit for resources to support working with disabled children and young people. www.childrenssociety.org.uk

Department for Education and Skills/Department of Health (2007) *Good Practice Guidance on Working with Parents with a Learning Disability.* London: DES/DoH.

Honey, P. and Mumford, A. (1982) *The Honey and Mumford Learning Styles Questionnaire*, consisting of 80 questions, is reasonably accessible within Learning and Development departments, and can be explored on www.peterhoney.com and many other websites refer to the materials.

Honey, P. and Mumford, A. (2006) The Learning Styles Questionnaire: 80-item Version. Maidenhead: Peter Honey Publications.

Lee-Foster, A. (2008) *Capacity to Communicate Training Toolkit*. London: Sense. Although designed for supporting advocacy and communication with deaf blind people, this toolkit contains helpful information and good practice useful for communicating with people who have a range of impairments. www.sense.org.uk

Mencap www.mencap.org.uk. Includes a 'Make it Clear' guide to making easy read information and suggestions about different ways of communicating with people with profound and multiple learning difficulties.

Morris, J. (2002) *A Lot to Say: A Guide for Social Workers, Personal Advisors and Others Working with Disabled Children and Young People with Communication Impairments*. London: Scope.

Morrison, T. (1993) *Staff Supervision in Social Care*. Harlow: Longman.

Morrison, T. (2001) *Staff Supervision in Social Care*. Brighton: Pavillion. Explores how our learning styles impact on our behaviour, how we can be trapped by our preferences into unproductive behaviours, and how to manage this.

Morrison, T. (2007) 'Emotional intelligence, emotion and social work: Context, characteristics, complications and contribution.' *British Journal of Social Work 37*, 2, 245–63.

Morrison, T. (2010) 'The strategic leadership of complex practice.' *Leigh (2009) Longitudinal Study of Australian Children University of Sydney and Canberra's Australian National University. Canberra: Australian National University.*, 312–29.

National Children's Bureau (2008) *How to Involve Children and Young People with Communication Impairments in Decision-Making*. London: NCB. www.participationworks. org.uk

Plain English. For more information on plain English, including an A to Z of alternative words, see www.plainenglish.co.uk

CHAPTER 5

Exploring Personal Preferences

Introduction

Explorations of diversity frequently concentrate on the obvious and visible ways in which we differ; the primary characteristics, as these are often the areas which cause social workers the most anxiety. However, the secondary characteristics can also have a very strong influence on how well workers engage with service users and whether their interventions are successful. Understanding our own learning style is a pre-requisite to effective engagement, whether or not the other person differs from us, and learning style is one of the ways in which difference impacts on social work. However, there are other differences that can give a bias to how we respond to the world and knowledge of these other characteristics enables us to communicate more effectively and celebrate diversity, especially in relation to those characteristics that we do not have ourselves.

The following chapter is based on Carl Jung's Psychological Types (1921/1971), which have been further developed by Isobel Myers and Katherine Briggs (1987, first published 1962), and David Keirsey (1978, 1998). We have taken the concepts as outlined by these writers and developed and explored them as they apply to social work. These writers use the term 'preference' in a very particular way. This chapter sets out our understanding of the pairs of preferences described by Jung, and Myers and Briggs (1987).

Understanding preferences

Introductory exercise

- Write your name in full.

- Now write it again using the other hand.

- How legible was the signature first time around?

- How legible was it the second time?

- What did it feel like doing it with the usual hand?

- What did it feel like doing it with the 'wrong' hand?

- What does this tell you about how it feels to do something against your natural inclination?

In writing their name the first time, some people will have preferred to use their left hand, others their right. When the opposite hand is used, the writing may not be legible or could be mirror writing. Equally, perhaps the result the second time is good, but it took much longer. A few people are ambidextrous and write equally well (or indeed equally badly!) with either hand. In general left-handed people are more ambidextrous because they live in a world where the majority of people are right-handed, so may have had to practice right-handed skills whether they wanted to or not. Indeed in the past children were forced to write with their right hands and were punished if they used the left hand. We now recognise that left handedness is simply a preference, and not something that requires correction.

In describing how it feels, most people will say that writing with their preferred hand feels natural, it comes easily and they do not have to think about it. Writing with the non-preferred hand is often described as awkward, it requires concentration and it is not as fluent. So it is with the other preferences explored below. The preferred styles are done fluently and without the need for thought. The non-preferred style needs thinking about. However, just because it is a preference, it does not mean that a person is good at it; people can still write poorly and illegibly with their preferred hand. Conversely, even if it is not their preferred style some people can still do it well, writing beautifully with their non-preferred hand.

Because each of us has a preferred way of doing things, we do it that way more often and so the preferred way quickly becomes the most skilled way. It also becomes part of our habitual way of doing things, a well-rehearsed cognitive chain, in which the thinking and feeling links are hardly noticed. It is in this sense that the word 'preference' is used throughout this chapter. Jung and Myers–Briggs describe preferences as about both what goes on in our heads and the way we behave.

Pairs of preferences

Jung and Myers–Briggs suggest that many of our preferences are innate, as with left and right handedness. As we grow, we mostly reinforce our handedness and other preferences. The more we practice our preferred way of doing things, the more skilled we become at our preference.

'Preference + practice = competence' (Taylor and Gast 2003)

However, we also learn to use the other hand for some tasks. We need to work with both hands, but tend to develop one preferred hand to a much higher level of skill. So it is with our other preferences.

The preferences explored are shown in Table 5.1.

Table 5.1 Preferences

Function	Preferences	
How people gain their energy	Extravert	Introvert
How people experience the world	Sensing (evidence based)	Intuition (ideas based)
How people make choices	Thinking	Feeling
How people check progress	Judging (just so)	Perceiving (okay so far)

These are explored in full later in the chapter. The ultimate aim for those using personality types is to gain a picture of the person on all four dimensions and understand how together the functions are connected in a larger system of psychological processes, but this is beyond the scope of this book (see Further reading and resources for suggestions for exploring these in greater detail).

An exploration

The model is based on juxtaposing two aspects of personality style. It looks at the differences which a preference in one of the aspects will highlight and the implications of this. The aspects are abbreviated to single letters which are:

E and I – for Extravert and Introvert

S and N – for Sensing and iNtuition

T and F – for Thinking and Feeling

P and J – for Perceiving and Judging.

In each of these pairings, Jung called the opposite to the preference the shadow side. The shadow side of the preference is less skilled, is likely to cause more stress when being employed, and may well result in awkward and even damaging behaviour. Being aware of somebody's preferences and when they have been thrown into using their shadow side has two benefits. First, it will help a worker provide an appropriate response to managing that behaviour, and second, find a way to avoid tipping the service user over into those behaviours.

The four pairs of preferences described

Extravert/introvert (E/I) pair of preferences – How we get energy

Extraversion and introversion are about where we focus our attention, where we get our energy from and how we become revitalised. These preferences explore how we interact with the world and with other people.

EXTRAVERT

Extraverts gain energy from being with people. They like people, parties and crowds. They are gregarious, sociable and expressive, looking outwards to others more than inwards to themselves. They feel the need to have people around them, becoming revitalised and energised by the company of others. They can become depressed if deprived of interactions with other people. This preference means they may quickly become socially skilled or well versed in the norms of their particular group. Peers therefore can be influential and they know themselves through their interaction with others. They will have lots of friends, but these might be quite superficial and short-term, being part of gangs or groups who come together fairly loosely. Because they are comfortable and skilled in groups, they can more easily learn in this situation and respond to the dominant culture of the group.

Extraverts are also in tune with the external environment, being aware of what is going on and alert to people around them. They like to communicate through talking and work their ideas out through the talking process. It could be said that they do not know what they are thinking until they have said it. In groups they may appear loud and chatty, and may find it very difficult to restrain themselves from commenting on what is going on.

Mature extraverts enjoy and need some time to themselves, but are likely to become lonely and experience a 'power drain' if cut off from human kind for any length of time. For some, just a day away from people will leave them hungry for company.

Extraverts appear to be the majority in western cultures, so set the norm for gregariousness and sociability.

Case study

Sanjay and his wife, Priti, came to the UK from India 60 years ago when they were both in their early 20s. Although they never had children they always had a wide circle of friends and were constantly busy and involved in the community. Once into their 80s, Sanjay and Priti's circle of friends began to dwindle, they didn't get out as much as they used to and their health began to deteriorate. They left their big house and moved into a flat across town. Sadly, just six weeks after the move, Priti became ill suddenly and died shortly after.

During their married life Priti had always been the one to do the shopping and cooking, and Sanjay now found himself having to learn to do these things. He also found the new area difficult to adjust to, and had lost touch with friends who used to call in on a regular basis before the move. Sanjay asked for some help and following an assessment a support worker came for a few hours each week to help him. Although he managed well and soon became more independent of the worker's help, it was clear all was not well. She noticed Sanjay became quieter and more subdued each week and began to worry he was simply going to 'give up'.

Then Sanjay's social worker arranged for him to attend a local day centre. It was within walking distance of his home, so Sanjay could drop in whenever he wanted, and stay all day if he liked. Over the next few weeks Sanjay often went to the drop-in sessions, he joined several of the clubs based at the centre, and had even begun to volunteer in the café there. On her next visit Sanjay's social worker was amazed to see the change in him; not only was he chatty and sociable, but he was making plans for the future and really seemed to be enjoying life again. It was almost as though he had 'woken up' at last. She realised this was due to enabling Sanjay to respond to his extrovert preference.

INTROVERT

Introverts gain energy from their own company, drawing from an inner world. Solitary activities are essential and they learn from reflection. They like people, but want to control the amount of time they spend with others. They can become overwhelmed in crowds and tend to avoid large gatherings.

Introverts replenish their inner energy by spending time on their own. They look more inwards to themselves than outwards to others. Being on their own is deeply satisfying and a place where they can find themselves again, recharging for a return to the fray. Introverts often like people, and tend to have fewer but closer and long lasting friends.

Introverts can experience extraverts 'en masse', as loud, demanding and exhausting. In a group work setting they are more likely to say little, and at break time withdraw to a corner and talk more intensively with one or two people.

Keirsey and Bates (1978) found about 25 per cent of the population to be introverts, so as a minority introverts can be made to feel that their shyness is a problem, rather than something to enjoy and celebrate. Inevitably most will have been schooled in groups and some learn to cope by becoming socially competent introverts, hiding in the crowd or inside their own heads whilst apparently present in class. Some become closet introverts because their work or school environment demands they display extravert behaviour rather than being able to be open about their preference.

In terms of social work interaction they may respond best to one-to-one work.

Case study

As part of a plan to support Marta to care for her three children, she was offered a place on a 'parenting programme' at the local Family Centre. Marta wasn't very keen – she is a quiet, rather shy person who finds going to new places difficult. She was worried what might happen if she refused, though, so agreed to go.

On her first day Marta was dismayed to find the programme wasn't her meeting with a support worker as she had thought, but involved being in a group with nine other parents and two workers for the whole morning. Some of the others in the group were very assertive, which Marta found intimidating, and she found herself withdrawing, becoming less and less involved as the session went on. When the break came she quickly went outside and found somewhere she could be on her own.

By the end of the morning the other parents had decided Marta was unfriendly and 'stand-offish' – they had all had to overcome their feelings about being there, and couldn't understand why she couldn't do the same. The workers reported back to Marta's social worker that Marta hadn't really engaged with the group at all, and didn't seem to want what the programme had to offer.

Points to consider

- How would you have interpreted Marta's behaviour?

- What might be the implications for Marta if she left the group?

- What might be the implications for Marta if she stayed in the group?

- If somebody is that uncomfortable, how would you feel about them withdrawing from a group?

- If Marta left, how could you ensure she received the perceived benefits of group work?

- How do you work with somebody when what you perceive is a benefit to them goes completely against their preference?

With introverts, what you see is not the whole personality. They will not allow themselves to reveal their deepest thoughts and qualities except in a very safe environment, say with trusted friends. Introverts are comfortable with private study and one-to-one tuition, though many may have learned to deal with groups because of the nature of their education.

To compare these preferences, see Table 5.2.

Table 5.2 Comparison of E/I preferences

Adaptive – when doing the preference well	Maladaptive – when unskilled in the preference	Responds to:
Extravert		
• charming	• boastful	• groups
• enthusiastic	• intrusive	• peer pressure
• sociable	• loud	• excitement
Introvert		
• deep	• aloof	• one-to-one
• discreet	• inhibited	• close friends
• tranquil	• withdrawn	• reflection

IN THE SHADOW

Jung describes the 'shadow' as our less preferred behaviours. In terms of this preference, extraverts in their shadow might become withdrawn and isolated, even reclusive; for some, this may even have implications for their mental health. For introverts, the emotional effort of spending a lot of time being sociable may leave them exhausted and burnt out. In extreme cases, this may manifest itself in manic behaviour. Younger people and those who have not adapted well, or any of us when suddenly out of our depth, are all capable of finding that in some situations we behave clumsily.

Case study

Jason is a young offender. He is an introvert, trying to be extravert, coming across as boastful and intrusive, and behaving 'over the top'. He became involved with a local gang where he was uncomfortable because he did not understand the unwritten rules of acceptable group behaviour. This led him to be the clown in the group, in order to try to fit in. His offending had taken place when others in his gang took advantage of his awkwardness, and pushed him into offending behaviour.

To compound his difficulties, when working with him, the social worker directed him into a group where he again behaved in an outrageous way.

Points to consider 1

- What criteria should the worker use to decide the appropriate intervention?

- What work could be done with Jason to explore why he behaves in this way?

- What difference would it make if the worker's preference matched Jason's or was opposite to it?

- What work could be done to help Jason become confident in managing his own preference?

Points to consider 2

- Where do you think you are on an introvert–extravert continuum (Table 5.3)?

- Rate yourself along the continuum.

Table 5.3 The introvert–extravert continuum

Reflective	0 – 1 – 2 – 3 – 4 – 5 – 6 – 7 – 8 – 9 – 10	Active
Inward looking	0 – 1 – 2 – 3 – 4 – 5 – 6 – 7 – 8 – 9 – 10	Outward looking
Reserved	0 – 1 – 2 – 3 – 4 – 5 – 6 – 7 – 8 – 9 – 10	Sociable
Quiet	0 – 1 – 2 – 3 – 4 – 5 – 6 – 7 – 8 – 9 – 10	Expressive
Deep	0 – 1 – 2 – 3 – 4 – 5 – 6 – 7 – 8 – 9 – 10	Broad

- What does this tell you about how you engage with people?

- How do you manage yourself when working with people who have the opposite preference?

- What implications does this have for your practice?

Suggestions for exploring the extravert/introvert (E/I) preferences with service users

Encourage the service user to talk about their lifestyle, to see whether they get their energy from being in a group or being on their own. Incorporate some of the questions below into your discussion, building on some of the answers which they have given.

- What activities do you do?

- Do you prefer to do them with other people?

- Do you go out with a group?

- Do you get together with other people after activities?

- How do you feel when you are in a gang?

- How do you feel when you work on your own?

- What do you enjoy about planning things with your friends?

- Are you happy in crowds?

  ◦ Do you like going to football matches?

  ◦ Do you go to rock concerts?

- When do you feel happiest – on your own or with other people?

- What sort of reaction do you get from being with people?

- Do you get tired afterwards?

- Can you party until late?

- Would you describe yourself as shy?

- Do you get to know strangers easily?

- Do you have lots of friends that you meet in a group?

- Do you prefer to have one or two close friends?

- Are you happy in your own company?

The answers to these explorations should give you a good indication of whether the service user is an E or and I and ideas about the best way of engaging with them. Having asked the closed questions to get an understanding of the preference, follow them up with open questions to explore the preference more fully.

Extraverts will need:

- lots of outgoing action and variety

- the opportunity to talk through new tasks with others

- people around them and chances to interact.

Introverts will need:

- time for quiet concentration

- opportunities to work alone

- longer to open up and trust you

- individual communication.

Sensing/iNtuition (S/N) pair of preferences – How we experience and know about the world

When alert to the differences, it is relatively easy to observe extraverts and introverts in action; however, the difference between sensing and intuitive types is not always so apparent to the casual observer. Nevertheless, the differences have profound implications, both for learning styles and for the way people communicate with each other. Much of our education is based on sensing, and intuitive behaviour, like daydreaming, is not something that is encouraged.

SENSING

Sensing types think about their world more in terms of concrete facts, and less in terms of concepts and abstract ideas. They know about the world through the information they get from their five senses, telling them what is out there, in the here and now, present and detectable.

People cannot look accurately at the external world as it is and simultaneously imagine future possibilities. You have to do one, then the other. Sensing people prefer the former and so this tends to take precedence. Consequently sensing types become skilled at noticing and handling detail, they are usually accurate and do not miss much. They seek out the facts and order them in meaningful and useful ways. Sensing types thrive on hard sequential information. They enjoy both obtaining and using information. Complex detail adds to their understanding.

Because of their preferred way of knowing the world they develop expert sensing skills and are therefore well grounded in present reality. Sensing types are creative in a practical and adapting way, preferring to develop and refine existing models. The test for them is that a model works well and is of practical use in everyday life.

Sensing types ask for clarification and concrete facts, and can be bewildered if they are not forthcoming. They are content to leave the abstract to the intuitives. The drive is to know what you have to do in practice; it is not necessary to know *how* it works, in order to make it work effectively.

Case study

> She helped me get to a refuge, she sorted out my benefits, got me a grant for uniform. It was a real help. She supported me. In practical terms. Then we could sit down and think what it all meant. For me, for the kids. I would not have been able to do that if she had not done the practical stuff first. (Wiffin 2010, para 7.7, p.43)

Points to consider

- Why is this case study here?
- What is 'sensing' about it?
- How would you continue to work with this mother?

INTUITION

Intuitive types are concerned with ideas and concepts in their heads. They are imaginative and can generate future possibilities, and may be experienced as having their head in the clouds. Intuitives know about their world more in terms of abstract ideas and how things relate to each other, rather than through concrete facts.

Because of this tendency to be absorbed in the inner world, they miss out on the details of the present external world around them, needing only sufficient detail to feed their imagination; then they stop looking. They tend to take the essence from the real world, and then work with an abstract idea about the world, rather than the evidence from their five senses. They like and create metaphors and can be easily drawn into fantasy. Intuitives respond to ideas and future possibilities with increasing energy. They rely on the sensing types to deal with the details of the real world.

Imaginative and inventive, intuitives see how things might be different. They must first understand the basics of how things fit together but will become bored with lots of detail. They are the designers, and the strategic planners. Success depends upon sufficient grounding in reality to make it happen, but they will not to be bound by present understanding and received wisdom.

IN THE SHADOW

If their preference is not well developed, then sensing types can be dull and obsessive about what they know and in their shadow can be terrified of their own fantasies. For intuitives, in their shadow they can be rendered almost catatonic by detail which they find overwhelming.

Table 5.4 Comparison of S/N preferences

Adaptive – when doing the preference well	Maladaptive – when unskilled in the preference	Responds to:
Sensing type		
• pragmatic	• dull	• detailed facts
• precise	• fussy	• sequential steps
• detailed	• obsessive	• practice
Intuitive type		
• imaginative	• eccentric	• variety
• ingenious	• erratic	• ideas
• insightful	• unrealistic	• future possibilities

Points to consider

- Where do you think you are on the sensing–intuition continuum?

- Rate yourself along the continuum according to your preference (Table 5.5).

Table 5.5 The sensing–intuition continuum

New ideas	$0-1-2-3-4-5-6-7-8-9-10$	Facts
Imaginative concepts	$0-1-2-3-4-5-6-7-8-9-10$	Being practical down to earth
Anticipation	$0-1-2-3-4-5-6-7-8-9-10$	Active enjoyment
The future	$0-1-2-3-4-5-6-7-8-9-10$	The present
Hunches	$0-1-2-3-4-5-6-7-8-9-10$	Directions

- What does this tell you about how you make sense of the world?

- How do you manage yourself when working with people who have the opposite preference?

- What implications does this have for your practice?

Suggestions for exploring the sensing–intuition (S/N) preferences with service users

Encourage the service user to talk about how they know about the world, with a view to seeing whether they seem to like facts and information and rely on what they can see and touch in the here and now (**sensing**).

Alternatively, do they seem to prefer ideas, imagination, and thinking about how things could be in the future, with perhaps a poor attention to detail (**intuitive**)?

Pay attention to language; listen out for a predominance of concrete words or abstract words.

Incorporate some of the questions below into your discussion.

- Are you interested in the details of how engines work?

- Do you take things to pieces to see how they are put together?

- If I give you some detailed directions, are you good at taking them in?

- Do you daydream a lot?

- Do you like science fiction?

- How easily can you imagine your life being different?

- Do you like to be aware of what is going on around you?

- Do you think about the future?

  ○ How often?

  ○ How enjoyable is that?

The answers to these explorations should give you a good indication of whether the service user is an S or and N and ideas about the best language and approach to use with them. Having asked the closed questions to get an understanding of the preference, follow them up with open questions to explore the preference more fully.

Thinking/feeling pair of preferences (T/F) – How we give value to things and people around us and therefore how we make decisions about our actions

Jung described how, when we think or feel about something, it is we who are projecting our thoughts/feelings onto that object. The colour or hardness of a stone is a property of the stone. Our thoughts and feelings about the colour or hardness of a stone come from us, and represent the value we place upon it. Others may think differently and therefore place a different value upon it. What we decide to do about the stone will arise from our thoughts and feelings about it.

This is the essence of cognitive behavioural work. We can change our thoughts and feelings and therefore our actions, but the emphasis between thinking and feeling will be different for different people:

- Thinking types rely principally on their thinking to act.

- Feeling types rely principally on their feelings to act.

For these preferences Keirsey and Bates (1978) found that the population was divided about 50–50; however, Myers–Briggs (1987) found that more women had a preference for feeling and men for thinking.

THINKING

Thinking types rely on arguments and logical thinking to arrive at an opinion or in deciding how to act. On balance, what they feel has less weight than the force of the argument. They do what is sensible. In terms of the learning cycle, they will be good at analysis. If in the mind of the thinker it makes sense, then it will determine how they choose to behave.

Thinking types use more thinking words, such as: 'on balance…', 'I think…'; 'my argument…'. Their sentences are often constructed like arguments or reasoning something out: 'if'; 'therefore'; 'because of'.

Just because thinking types rely on their own logic, it does not follow that they will necessarily have poorly developed feelings. Many will take account of their feelings in coming to a conclusion. Others may have poorly developed awareness of feelings and act only according to the balance of the facts. Thinking types may struggle to deal with other people's feelings and try to avoid displays of emotions. They will tend to speak their minds and are surprised if others are upset by this. They can act irrespective of others' feelings.

In a cognitive behavioural approach, for thinking types especially, changed thinking leads to changed behaviour. Matching the style of language and cognitive process is concomitant to achieving rapport. Asking a thinking type what they felt about their actions is the same as asking a left-handed person to write down their thoughts with their right hand. For thinking types actions follow thought, so the focus of work must be on helping them to see the sense of behaving differently and establishing alternative reasoning when solving problems.

FEELING

Many feeling types have well-developed sensitivity to others' feelings, and will prefer harmony to conflict. Achievement of harmony and smoothing the path is often the overriding concern in how they behave and what they feel they should do. The impression they make on others touches the very heart of their desire to like and to be liked. To say that feelings are not important or cannot usefully be worked with is a slap in the face to someone who relates to the world through their feelings.

Feeling types use and respond to feeling language (both emotional and kinaesthetic) ' feels good to me'; 'made an impact on me'; 'touch and go'; 'I am unhappy about…'; 'I care to…'; 'I felt like a stroll'; 'a rough deal'. Their language is often sprinkled with kinaesthetic simile and metaphor.

Some immature feeling types are less sensitised to others, or their awareness of others is blunted by an acute awareness of their own feelings. They have yet to develop empathy for others. These people can act only according to the emotion of the moment, or the feelings that consume them.

In a cognitive behavioural approach, for feeling types especially, changed feelings lead to changed behaviour. Matching the style of language and cognitive process is concomitant to achieving rapport. Asking a feeling type what they thought about their actions is like asking a left-handed person to write down their feelings with their right hand. For feeling types, whose actions follow their feelings, the focus of work must be on helping them to develop empathy and to use appropriate thinking when solving problems.

Case study

> She cared you know. I was not just a case, but a person. It was something about her. I don't know. We had our ups and downs, and she could get cross, but I knew that she cared, and I kept coming back to that. (Wiffin 2010, para 7.5, p.41)

Points to consider

- Why is this case study here?
- What is 'feeling' about it?
- How would you continue to work with this service user?

Table 5.6 Comparison of thinking–feeling preferences

Adaptive – when doing the preference well	Maladaptive – when unskilled in the preference	Responds to:
Thinking types		
• lucid	• argumentative	• justice
• objective	• intolerant	• analysis
• succinct	• cold	• principles
Feeling types		
• appreciative	• evasive	• harmony
• considerate	• vague	• values
• tactful	• hypersensitive	• caring

IN THE SHADOW

Some thinking types may take insufficient account of the impact of their behaviour on others. They can be overcome and deeply upset when their feelings seem out of control, and then be unable to act. Some feeling types may be driven by the need for harmony now rather than what is sensible in the long term. They may be confused by arguments and not know what to do or which way to turn.

Case study

Over the previous two years Mrs Malone had watched her husband develop severe Alzheimer's and deteriorate rapidly. He went into residential care, then into hospital and at the time of his death could no longer recognise anybody, could not put together a coherent sentence and was behaving in a very demanding way. Throughout this process Mrs Malone remained very rational and in control of her own emotions and tried to treat her husband as though he, too, was still rational.

After his death she asked for help, as she too was no longer remembering things as well as she wished and was becoming frail. She kept saying that she was fine and coping, but it was obvious to others that she was not.

During one visit by her social worker, whilst being pushed very gently to consider what would be the best for her future, as she was now having trouble cooking for herself and managing the home, Mrs Malone suddenly started screaming. She dropped to the floor, rolling around and thumping her fists like a two-year-old having a temper tantrum.

As a thinking type she had suppressed her feelings for so long that when she did let them out, they controlled her rather than her being able to control them. (Personal account given to author)

Points to consider

- Where do you think you are on the thinking–feeling continuum?

- Rate yourself along the continuum according to your preference for making decisions based on the factors in Table 5.7.

Table 5.7 The thinking–feeling continuum

Head	$0 - 1 - 2 - 3 - 4 - 5 - 6 - 7 - 8 - 9 - 10$	Heart
Critical	$0 - 1 - 2 - 3 - 4 - 5 - 6 - 7 - 8 - 9 - 10$	Appreciative
Analytic	$0 - 1 - 2 - 3 - 4 - 5 - 6 - 7 - 8 - 9 - 10$	Empathetic
Precise	$0 - 1 - 2 - 3 - 4 - 5 - 6 - 7 - 8 - 9 - 10$	Persuasive
Likely to use objective criteria	$0 - 1 - 2 - 3 - 4 - 5 - 6 - 7 - 8 - 9 - 10$	Likely to use subjective criteria

- What does this tell you about how you make choices?

- How do you manage yourself when working with people who have the opposite preference?

- What implications does this have for your practice?

Suggestions for exploring the thinking–feeling (T/F) preferences with service users

Encourage the service user to talk about how they consider information and make choices.

Pay attention to language, listening out for a predominance of thinking or feeling words.

Incorporate some of the questions below into your discussion, building on some of the answers which they have given in response to the pictures. Having asked the closed questions to get an understanding of the preference, follow them up with open questions to explore the preference more fully.

- Do you try to think things through clearly?
- Do you find you think in terms of 'this and then that'?
- Do you notice how you are feeling a lot of the time?
- Do you have to have a reason to do things?
- Do you do something because you think it is right or because it feels right?
- Is it more important to think things through or to respond according to how you feel?
- Why do you keep appointments with our organisation when you do?
- How would you decide on:
  ○ How to spend a lottery win?
  ○ What car you might like?

Thinking people need you to:

- encourage them with logical arguments
- respond to their ideas

- be fair, firm and tough-minded

- encourage them to analyse problems

- take them towards the most logical outcomes.

Feeling people need you to:

- respond to their values as much as their thoughts

- encourage them to see the effects of their choices for themselves and others

- be sympathetic and provide praise

- be interested in the person behind the actions.

Just-so/perceiving pair of preferences (J/P) – How we determine our progress in the world

The just-so and perceiving preferences are concerned with how we determine our progress in the world. Jung and Myers–Briggs talk about judging and perceiving; however, the word 'judging' may be confusing in organisations associated with the justice and care systems, so we feel 'just-so' is a better description for this preference.

JUST-SO

Just-so types evaluate themselves and the world against targets and time. They like things in their place; structured and organised. They are likely to be anxious if not on time or track. Nothing pleases a just-so type more than to foreclose, or finish a project. They can even ignore a present predicament in order to maintain targets. Being late is the ultimate disgrace. Anxiety can be very high if not on schedule and on target. A tidy mind and a tidy world are satisfying. They rely on preparation, planning, schedules, targets and organisation to get objectives achieved.

Whilst just-so types can be highly organised and effective, they can also meet their objectives with little awareness of the developing needs of others or the changing situation. Evaluation is made after the event. They can be irritated by the apparent laxity and 'take it as it comes' of perceiving types.

PERCEIVING

Perceiving types evaluate against present state of play and are responsive to the present situation of people and their immediate needs. They notice what is going on around them now, like to keep things open and do not want to foreclose. They are frequently relaxed time keepers and their approach to life seems unstructured.

Perceiving types like to keep their options open, perceiving the present state of play and the next required move. They probe the options at any point. They are aware (intuitively or sensingly) of what is going on around them and rely on that incoming knowledge to take one of the many options they see as next best step.

Because of this they are responsive to the needs of others and developing situations. They take pleasure in situations evolving around them and finding their way through is fun. They are excellent people to have around at a time of crisis as they rise to the situation. Deadlines, orderliness and planning are of much less concern.

In a world that is increasingly organised and time driven, they can seem disorganised. Yet proficient perceiving types come up with the goods, just in time, and the goods that are actually required by the situation. They are easily irritated by schedules and tidy, highly structured organisation. They have a high tolerance to disarray and mayhem. Playfulness is never far away.

Table 5.8 Comparison between just-so and perceiving preferences

Adaptive – when doing the preference well	Maladaptive – when unskilled in the preference	Responds to:
Just-so types		
• efficient	• compulsive	• organisation
• well-planned	• deadlines	• deadlines
• responsible	• rigid	• control
Perceiving types		
• adaptable	• procrastinate	• curiosity
• easy going	• unreliable	• spontaneity
• flexible	• scattered	• openness

IN THE SHADOW

Just-sos can be frozen when faced with irredeemable chaos. Perceiving types can find themselves unable to function where the organisation is rigid and procedures strictly imposed.

Case study

Suzanne's social worker, Rosa, was due to take her for an appointment to look around a sheltered housing scheme. They were meeting at Suzanne's house the next morning. Rosa was a just-so, and recognising that Suzanne (a perceiving type) was always late, gave her an arrival time 10 minutes earlier than necessary, to ensure they got to their appointment on time. Suzanne, knowing that Rosa put a lot of emphasis on good timekeeping, made an extra effort to be ready for the agreed time (not 10 minutes late as she would normally have been). Rosa was then caught out because she was not expecting Suzanne to be on time! They were both able to laugh about it, but it developed a far greater understanding of each other's approach to timekeeping. (Account given to author)

> How does she think her (the social worker's) constant lateness makes me feel? Worthless? Unimportant? Yes. If I am late – well, that's different. They do not understand then.' (Wiffin 2010, para 6.5, p.34)

Points to consider

- Where do you think you are on the just-so–perceiving continuum (Table 5.9)?

- Rate yourself along the continuum according to how you organise yourself:

Table 5.9 The just-so–perceiving continuum

Organised	$0 - 1 - 2 - 3 - 4 - 5 - 6 - 7 - 8 - 9 - 10$	Flexible
Structured	$0 - 1 - 2 - 3 - 4 - 5 - 6 - 7 - 8 - 9 - 10$	Responsive
Driven by deadlines	$0 - 1 - 2 - 3 - 4 - 5 - 6 - 7 - 8 - 9 - 10$	Driven by discoveries
Deliberate	$0 - 1 - 2 - 3 - 4 - 5 - 6 - 7 - 8 - 9 - 10$	Spontaneous
Responding to predictability	$0 - 1 - 2 - 3 - 4 - 5 - 6 - 7 - 8 - 9 - 10$	Responding to crises

- What does this tell you about how you make/determine your progress in the world?

- How do you manage yourself when working with people who have the opposite preference?

- What implications does this have for your practice?

Suggestions for exploring the just-so–perceiving (J/P) preferences with service users

Encourage the service user to talk about how they organise their time and respond to deadlines.

Incorporate some of the questions below into your discussion. Having asked the closed questions to get an understanding of the preference, follow them up with open questions to explore the preference more fully.

- Are you good at getting to places on time?

- Do you plan what you are going to do each day?

- Do you plan your day or do you just let things happen?

- Do you take a list when you go shopping?

- Can you cope with lots of loose ends?

- Do you like to know what is happening at the end of a story from the start?

- Are you happy when things just happen and you go with the flow?

- Do you prefer to make things happen according to your plan?

- Would you describe yourself as more easy-going than organised?

Judging (just-so) people need:

- opportunities to plan and follow through the plan

- a work schedule

- chances for work to be completed

- the opportunity to work without interruptions.

> **Perceiving people need:**
>
> • to be allowed them to find their own pace
>
> • to be encouraged to use their awareness of what is happening now
>
> • a flexible approach
>
> • a push to take action
>
> • pressure from you to organise and complete a task.

Conclusion

This is a brief introduction to the complexity of personal preferences. In encountering someone with a different preference we are likely to find them irritating. They pay attention to different things, they use different language, behave differently. Looking at these preferences might help us to see:

- when somebody needs the stimulation of others around or might need to be quiet and on their own

- whether they might need to go into a lot of practical detail or can only see the big picture

- whether they might be able to deal with feelings, or to think logically about what is best

- when they might be easily distracted by crises and whatever comes up, rather than being able to settle to a structured and diaried existence.

Reflections

Can you identify your own preferences? Some may be very strong but others may be less so. Sometimes it is easier to spot the preferences in those around you. Can you ask others to see if they can identify your preferences?

It has been shown that as people grow older they often increase their skills in their least preferred styles, although a clear preference remains. Younger and inexperienced people tend therefore to show more extremes in their preferred styles and associated skills, which obviously has implications for working with younger people. Jung also believed that as people grew older they sought to explore their less preferred styles. As will become clear, people acting in their less preferred styles are less fluent and skilled in their behaviours, which is relevant when working with older people.

> Family members said there were times when there was a 'clash of personalities' or 'she (the social worker) did not like me'.

How much of what we describe as clash of personalities is really not understanding somebody else's preferences about how they operate in the day-to-day world?

Further reading and resources

Gast, L. Linda Gast training@lindagast.co.uk has a version of the questionnaire (called the Gast Taylor Inventory [GTi]) which is available as part of training courses and team development workshops.

Keirsey, D. and Bates, M. (1978) *Please Understand Me: Character and Temperament Types.* California: Prometheus Nemesis. This book has a version of a questionnaire that would allow you to get a more detailed understanding of your own preferences.

Myers, I. and Briggs, K. There are many qualified Myers–Briggs practitioners who can administer the questionnaire, including the opportunity to do the American version on-line www.MyersBriggsReports.com. There is usually a charge involved.

Myers, I. and McCaulley, M.H. (1985) *Manual: A Guide to the Development and Use of the Myers Briggs Type Indicator.* Palo Alto, CA: Consulting Psychologists Press. www.MyersBriggsReports.com.

CHAPTER 6
A Diversity Awareness Model

We tend to assume that if someone has some sort of 'difference', whatever it is, that they will know about that difference, and will understand and appreciate the significance of the difference. For many people that is so, but for some there is no good reason why they should have any knowledge about their 'difference', for as far as they are concerned they are the norm and there is no reason to know about norms. This model looks at some of the stages which people can go through in developing an understanding of their own diversity. It also helps to unpick what can happen to both individuals and organisations as they learn about issues of diversity, and the impact that this learning can have.

The model introduced in this chapter is drawn from several different sources; Carter (1990), who developed six stages of white racial consciousness, and Atkinson, Morten and Sue (1989) who identified 'Five Statuses of Black Racial Identity'. These two approaches use different language, but they align with each other quite closely and are helpful in developing a broader understanding of how people comprehend diversity. This model can also be put alongside the transition curve (Figure 6.1) which was itself developed from the bereavement curve (Kübler-Ross 1969) and describes stages of realisation and the feelings that can accompany each stage as a person goes through a transition.

But first it's important to distinguish between transition and change. Bridges (1991) describes the difference between the two in this way:

> It isn't the changes that do you in, it's the transitions. Change is not the same as transition. *Change* is situational: the new site, the new boss, the new team roles, the new policy. *Transition* is the psychological process people go through to come to terms with the new situation. Change is external, transition is internal.

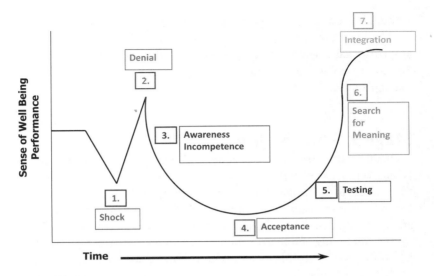

Figure 6.1 The transition curve

If we relate these concepts to developing an awareness of diversity (going through a transition) it becomes easier to understand the way in which the process of becoming aware of difference evokes emotive reactions in individuals. It is the interface between people at different stages in the model that can cause upset and annoyance.

The diversity awareness model can be depicted as a five-stage process (Figure 6.2).

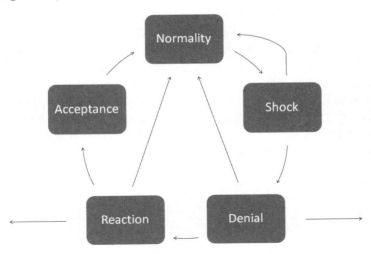

Figure 6.2 The Diversity Awareness Model

Although presented as a cycle, people can go back to their 'normality' at any point and may opt out of moving forward, choosing to stay at any particular stage for what appears to them to be very good reasons. For some people, moving right around the cycle is too demanding or uncomfortable.

Stage 1 – 'normality'

To begin with, most of us assume that who we are and how we operate is relatively normal, and that if we think and behave in a particular way, then others to will think and behave similarly; our 'story of the world'. If we have grown up in a culture where boys will be boys, and girls are very different, then the expectations are that the genders will be treated differently and there is no problem about that. The fact that there is a difference in treatment is not even noticed as anything particular, as that is just how life is. Just as there is no reason to assume that a woman will have noticed sexism, so a minority ethnic person may not have consciously experienced racism. The diversity is operating at an unconscious incompetence level, of not recognising that there are even issues to be addressed, so therefore, nothing can be done about it. This may be expressed as: 'I don't know what all the fuss is about. I have never experienced…' The socialisation process is not noticed for what it is and there will be a lack of understanding about people who are seeing the world differently.

In an organisation, whoever has been the predominant work force represents the 'norm', and there is no reason to treat anyone any differently, as 'we are all okay around here'. There tends to be a need to reinforce conformity, and there is a lack of knowledge about differences. If diversity issues raise their heads, they can be passed to a specialist; for example, providing aids for a disabled person so that they can then be expected to do the same job as everybody else. For somebody from a minority group to succeed, they probably need to be functioning at a level high on Maslow's hierarchy of needs (see Figure 6.3), and focused on self-actualisation. They usually have to be more like the members of the dominant group than the dominant group are in reality, and have to fully meet organisational requirements to fit in.

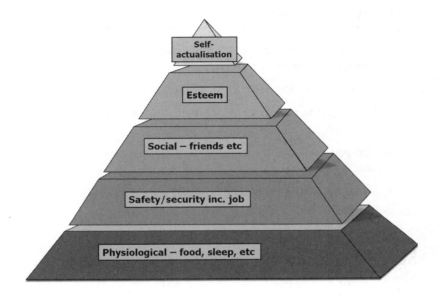

Figure 6.3 Maslow's Hierarchy of Needs (1954)

Case study

When working with Anil, a learning disabled young person, Samuel, his social worker, asked him if he had ever been bullied. Anil said he had not.

A few days later Samuel spoke with a classroom assistant who worked at Anil's school. She told him that she travels on the same bus as Anil and regularly saw him being targeted by other young people on the bus. She said she had seen him being taunted, pushed, and spat at, and was aware of at least two occasions when Anil had got off the bus before his usual stop to escape these unwanted, and unwarranted attentions.

When Samuel next saw Anil he reminded him of their previous conversation, when Anil had denied being bullied, and of the new information from the classroom assistant. Anil agreed the things she had described had happened, but said that those sorts of things were just part of his usual life. He expected them, was used to them, and didn't regard them as being bullied.

Points to consider

- What does this example tell you about where Anil is on the diversity awareness model?

- What might you do to help him understand his experiences?

- Where is the classroom assistant on the diversity awareness model?

- Do you think this impacted on her passivity in the face of Anil's experiences?

- How might she be helped to move forward and be more proactive?

Stage 2 – shock

At some stage something may upset this equilibrium, and individuals and organisations can begin to question their worldview as it relates to a particular aspect of diversity. This may be a change of circumstances; beginning social work training, moving to a different area, into a different job, mixing with a different set of people. Alternatively, it may be the impact of a change of perception; something that has been read, something that somebody has said, an experience, which in some way has had an impact. This may be expressed in a questioning way: 'I hadn't realised that people might see it like that,' and can cause a large amount of discomfort about their view of themselves and/or the view of the world. For women, it might be noticing that there are not many of them in managerial positions in most organisations, so perhaps the glass ceiling does exist. For minority ethnic people it may be the realisation that their daily experiences are different – the way they are looked at, the treatment they receive, the jokes they are expected to tolerate and the indications that they are lesser or at least very different from white people. For somebody who is disabled this might trigger some serious questioning about why they are not able to access the same range of opportunities as non-disabled people, particularly in public life; access to buildings, the provision of hearing loops, mainstream educational opportunities. For somebody with a different sexual orientation, the reaction may well be because they are not able to display their relationship in public.

These 'light bulb moments' do not occur across the spectrum of diversity; they only happen about one subject at a time. People can become very attuned to one area of discriminatory behaviour but oblivious to it in another. The shock has to happen for each area of learning and, depending on exposure to the different areas, may or may not register with each individual.

For an organisation, the shock may come from somebody pointing out legislative requirements, finding themselves at an employment tribunal, or the development of internal procedures, or it may just be a challenge from a staff group from within. The shock can be quite traumatic to the whole organisation and lead to a great deal of uncertainty about how to respond.

Case study

Petra had been working in a children and families team for a year. In two of the families she worked with the parents had learning difficulties. Petra believed she had taken account of this in her work with them, for instance, she ensured that when she wrote to them, she kept her language simple and used size 16 font. Petra then had a chance to go on a training course to increase her knowledge about working with parents who have learning disability. What she heard there really shocked her – that parents with learning difficulties are 15 to 50 times more likely than other parents in the community to have their children removed from them and placed in care (Department of Health and Department for Education and Skills 2007), and only 52 per cent of parents with learning difficulties looked after their children (Emerson *et al.* 2005). She also heard that the number of parents with learning difficulties is on the increase, and yet their needs are not being adequately addressed by health and social services. She discovered that these parents face numerous barriers, including negative attitudes and stereotypes of parents who have learning disability, lack of coordination between children's and adult services, and practitioners not feeling properly equipped to work effectively with them.

Points to consider

- What range of reactions do you think Petra might have?
- What is your own range of reactions to this account?
- Can you relate this to another area of diversity where you have had this experience?

- What did you do about your reactions to that experience?

- What might you do to help yourself understand the areas of diversity which might still take you into 'shock'?

Stage 3 – denial

Shock is likely to lead straight into denial. 'We have always done things like this and it has never been a problem before.' The belief is that if we always do what we have always done, we will always get what we have always got, not recognising that the world has moved on. Circumstances have changed, the shock has caused a reaction and life cannot return as it was. Yet the overwhelming tendency for both organisations and individuals is to bury their heads in the sand and try to ignore the change. For women, there was a denial that they needed anything different to men. There was no recognition that the prime carer was likely to be the woman, so there would be different needs around working hours, flexible working years and cover for child sickness. 'If they can't work "properly" they should not be in the job.' For minority ethnic people the denial was again that they needed anything different. There was a lack of acknowledgement that the education system might have treated a minority ethnic person less fairly; therefore the fact that to achieve the same standard they might need a different sort of support mechanism to be provided, is ignored. In terms of the recognition of all types of difference, communication continues according to previous behaviours, with no appreciation that this might not be the most effective way for the communication to take place.

The denial stage may mean that behaviour tries to stick very rigidly to what has always been done before, which will lead to strong reactions in those who have started to develop their awareness.

Case study

Carla is deaf. She qualified as a social worker three years ago and has been working in her current team for six months. She is the first deaf worker in the team and from the start her colleagues were keen to demonstrate that they didn't treat her any differently because of her impairment. After a few weeks a number of difficulties began to arise. For instance, the lighting in the office was poor and seating arranged in cubicles, making lip reading and seeing facial expressions difficult. Team meetings often involved presentations with overheads, and Carla found it difficult to lip read and read the overheads at the same time and often missed bits. One colleague, who had a beard and a tendency to put his hand in front of his face, was particularly poor at ensuring that Carla could see him when he was talking.

The team also had a habit of going for lunch together once a week, but the nearby coffee house they frequented tended to have boisterous crowds with lots of extraneous noise, not an easy environment for Carla. She gradually felt more and more excluded, but didn't want to say anything in case she was seen as complaining. The team members believed that they had made 'reasonable adjustment' and perceived her to be unfriendly when she did not participate as fully as they thought she should.

Points to consider

- What range of reactions do you think the team members might have?

- What are the benefits to denying that there is a communication problem in this team?

- What is your own range of reactions to this account?

- Can you relate this to another area of diversity where you have experienced individual or collective denial?

- What could be done in response to that experience?

- What might you do to help yourself understand the areas of diversity which might still take you into 'denial'?

Stage 4 – reaction

The reactions to growing awareness can manifest themselves in many different ways, which will vary from individual to individual, but will also vary for each individual at different times. These can be anger, guilt, depression, disillusionment or even fear. For the person whose diversity is not being recognised, anger is perhaps the most common: 'How dare people treat me like this, and ignore my different needs?' For the person becoming aware of the difference, the anger can be expressed towards individuals, people in authority or those with power who are in a position to affect the behaviours of others. The anger can be vented against the particular individuals or the organisation as a whole. As organisations are particularly slow to learn and change, this level of anger and frustration can occasionally become a well-rehearsed and repetitive pattern of behaviour that an individual can get stuck in. For some people the anger can even be beneficial, as it means that others are in awe of them and they may be able to get away with behaviours that would not be tolerated in others.

Alternatively, the awareness can manifest itself in sadness and a desire to share that with others; or an overwhelming enthusiasm which is spread widely and can be contagious. The awareness can trigger a great deal of reading; of feminist writers, of black history, of different personality types and Jungian psychology, or whatever. This enthusiasm can be helpful for others around, but if they are at a different stage in the process the new awareness can be pushed away: 'It's just somebody on their hobby horse.'

A frequent response at this stage is to define the issue as too dangerous, and therefore stop saying anything about the subject unless somebody else has already said something and that has been seen to be alright. This often happens to social workers during training. They have begun to see that differences do impact on people's life experiences, but their own anxieties about 'getting it wrong' in front of other students, who they perceive to be more politically correct than themselves, or their tutors and practice teachers, who will be assessing their practice, means that areas of diversity are glossed over and avoided as much as possible. This can be noticed when a person at this stage pauses before they say anything, thinking about how to phrase their thoughts in an acceptable way. The pause is seen as an indicator of their discomfort with the subject, and the person experiencing the pause is likely to judge the level of the speaker's awareness critically.

This stage can be worked through quite quickly, for example, an awareness of the inequity of treatment of minority ethnic people can lead rapidly to an acceptance that something needs to be done, and some personal responsibility is taken to do something. But again, everybody is different, and if the learning style of the individual requires that they have to take apart their understanding of the world to incorporate this new knowledge, this might be thought to be too difficult, too demanding, not worth the bother, or 'not quite what I want to do at the moment'. This can leave the person stuck at the awareness stage for some considerable time. They know that things have to change, but cannot quite get around to the acceptance stage.

This stage of heightened awareness can be very satisfying for the person in it, because it gives them information power (see Chapter 1), stimulation, a trigger for further learning or particular insights that others do not have.

The organisation, with so many people working at so many different places in it, will continue to express the majority view rather forcibly. There will be pockets of awareness in the organisation and there may well be an intention to incorporate that awareness into the organisational norms, but somehow it falls into the 'too difficult' box, or there is too much else going on at the moment and it just does not quite reach the stage of acceptance and change. We know what we don't know (conscious incompetence), but are not quite sure how to move on from there. There is likely to be anger against the people who are seen to be rocking the boat.

Case study

Gilda is black and has dyslexia. Her early school experiences were negative and she has consistently had to overcome her fears and feelings about learning to succeed in her professional training. Written work is particularly stressful for her.

Gilda has a real talent for working with young people; they seem to trust her and recognise that she would 'do battle' on their behalf if necessary. She enjoyed her role as a personal adviser, seconded to a voluntary agency working with young people. The team was then disbanded, their work absorbed into the local authority leaving care team and Gilda moved across to this team.

This would not have been her team of choice as the work role required writing numerous court reports which she knew was not her strength. She set herself up with a voice activated laptop, but found the open-plan office environment was not conducive to using it as it picked up on all the extraneous noise.

Gilda requested to be allowed to work at home but her manager would not agree to this. He believed that by this stage of her career she ought to be able to manage the job requirements and was angry about having a member of staff who, he believed, needed to have all of her work checked before submission. He thought that now she had her laptop she ought to be able to manage; if he allowed her to work from home it would set a precedent and he implied that she was expecting too many allowances to be made.

Points to consider

- Why do you think the manager responded in this way? What might be the contributory factors to his reactions?

- What range of reactions do you think other team members might have?

- What is your own range of reactions to this account?

- What might be the independent impact of Gilda's race, her gender and her disability?

- What arrangements might enable Gilda to operate successfully in this team?

- What might you do to help yourself understand the areas of diversity which might still take you into 'reaction'?

Stage 5 – acceptance

We are all different. We accept this. At this stage we are willing to work together to develop a diverse working community and a more equitable organisation. But what do we need to do? Acceptance alone does not necessarily achieve a positive outcome. It could lead to complacency, or even collusion, and the behaviours could be interpreted as those of the 'normality' stage. Perhaps, indeed, there are some similarities, as it is a stage of rather more equanimity. We are at the point of conscious competence, when considered decisions can be made about what should be done for the best for all concerned, and consideration is given to all aspects of diversity. We haven't got it right yet; it is just a real appreciation that we have to move on and things cannot be left to drift back to unconscious incompetence.

For many people there will still be a propensity to 'get it wrong'. It is very difficult to change years of socialisation and education. Phrases are entrenched in our memories and have a propensity to come out at the most inappropriate time. It is a matter of accepting that most people, particularly our colleagues, do not intend to be '...ist'; it is more that they have not thought the issue through in enough depth, habits are hard to change, accepted language shifts at a very rapid pace, or they are embarrassed and awkward (see Chapter 2 for the model for understanding this). This is the time when we really need to be kind to each other. It is about taking personal ownership of the hurt which another person has caused us, and explaining why this is so. 'When you say that it makes me feel..., and then I...'

Organisationally there will still be the need for a great deal of debate, learning and modification of policies and practice guidelines, but perhaps there is a greater willingness from all concerned to learn from mistakes, and share the learning.

Case study

The aim of reaching the acceptance stage in our understanding of diversity is not for its own sake, but to achieve successful outcomes with service users.

> Our situation is unique (as is that of other families). Listen to what we need, don't assume you know.

> Good social workers really do want to help. They're creative, try to think round things, and think of the whole family.
>
> (Research comments made to author)

Final point to consider

> ...to promote diversity effectively, we need to stop doing the things that create barriers and start doing the things that break them down. (Audit Commission 2004)

Thoughts

These stages are not fixed. We can move backwards as well as forwards if something happens to make our views more entrenched. Just because we have developed awareness in one area of discrimination, it does not necessarily follow that we have even started on the exploration of another area. To get stuck at any one stage may have beneficial effects for some people, so they may chose not to move on. When we are dealing with some of our most established beliefs, which stem from all of our socialisation, we appear to move along the transition curve very slowly, so progression from one stage to another can be painful and reluctantly undertaken. Working with people who are at different stages can feel difficult, as we expect others to be able to make the same progress as we ourselves have made, and we can be intolerant of others who have not developed their thinking as far. It can also feel very annoying if some individuals or the organisation are moving more slowly than we think they should, or are becoming entrenched at different stages. All of this makes for a very complex management situation – but that happens anyway and this is simply a model for trying to make sense of what is happening to both individuals and the organisation!

Table 6.1 Diversity questionnaire

Points to consider

- This will require you to be really honest with yourself and may be quite painful, but could help with acknowledging the areas of diversity on which you might still need to focus. This might include admitting to attitudes that do not sit comfortably with your role as a social worker and the expectations placed on the profession.

- Some of these areas require you to be very brave, and you may wish to be cautious about whether you share and who you share it with. However, in order to develop, the more you can share the more you will learn and grow confident about your management of diversity.

STAGE 1 NORMALITY

What attitudes, prejudices and biases did you grow up with about areas of diversity? For example:

- The role of women

- The status of older people

- People with physical disabilities

- People with learning difficulties

- People with mental health issues

- Gay people

- Attitudes to people from different countries

- People from different faiths

- People who were considered eccentric

- People who are obese

- Any others, e.g. single parent families, people with HIV/Aids, standards of hygiene, class, gypsies/Roma, etc?

- How common were these attitudes, or could you recognise that those of your immediate family were different from those in your wider community?

STAGE 2 SHOCK

- At what point did you recognise that other people had different attitudes, prejudices and biases?

- How did you become aware of this?

- What was your reaction?

- Do members of your family hold attitudes, values or beliefs that are very different to yours, which you find difficult?

- In what areas of diversity have you not yet had the 'light bulb moment'? – i.e. that you don't quite understand what the differences entail and how they impact on people's lives (these might be very specific: particular areas of disability or particular religions, for example).

STAGE 3 DENIAL

- In what circumstances have you found yourself saying (or thinking):

  'I don't know what all the fuss is about.'

  'Why should they be treated any differently?'

  'What about my diversity…?'

  'Why can't we just treat everyone the same?'

- If you have heard other people saying these sorts of things, how have you responded?

- Are you more confident about challenging some areas of discrimination than others?

- What experiences have led to this difference?

- Are there other areas which you find easier to avoid or ignore and why do you think this might be?

STAGE 4 REACTION

- In what circumstances have you found yourself having a rant about how 'they' (whoever 'they' are) get preferential treatment?

- In what circumstances have you caught yourself having lapses into stereotypical thinking about groups?

  'They're all like that.'

  'What can you expect from them?'

- Why do you think it was these areas which triggered this reaction?

- When you caught yourself thinking or saying this, how did you react?

- How do you balance the conscious, professional reaction with your deep-seated, emotional reactions?

STAGE 5 ACCEPTANCE

- In what areas of diversity do you feel comfortable with your knowledge (or lack of it)?

- How is this demonstrated in your behaviours?

- How might you test whether other people would agree with your analysis?

- In what areas do you need to go back to your 'normality' stage and re-start your thinking?

- From these considerations, what areas do you need to work on?

- How do you plan to do this and who will help you?

Conclusions

This model enables us all to understand better the multiracial, multicultural society in which we live and could help us to appreciate the diversity which each person brings to any interaction. However, the potential for unconscious attitudes distorting the interaction are immense.

Organisations, like people, pass through stages of growth in their awareness of diversity, and their ability to encompass the change necessary to be fully inclusive. People in organisations have a responsibility to honestly evaluate their position in the model, and to work together to move themselves and the organisation on.

We each have personal responsibility to develop our awareness, which is a life-long journey, adding richness to our story of the world.

Issues from this chapter to discuss with your supervisor

The ultimate aim of this chapter would be for you to be able to discuss the details of the questionnaire openly and honestly with your supervisor and your colleagues. We acknowledge that this requires an environment of safety and trust, but it will only be when this exists that people will be able to make mistakes about diversity, acknowledge that they have got things wrong, and learn from this.

The more we understand each other's diversity, the more likely it is that this safe environment can be developed, in an atmosphere of mutual respect.

Further reading and resources

Helms, J.E. (1984) 'Towards a theoretical model of the effects of race on counselling: A black and white model.' *The Counselling Psychologist 12*, 153–65.

Leigh (2009) Longitudinal Study of Australian Children University of Sydney and Canberra's Australian National University. Canberra: Australian National University.

REFERENCES

Allen, H., Larsen, J., Bryan, K. and Smith, P. (2004) 'The social reproduction of institutional racism: Internationally recruited nurses' experiences of the British health service.' Radcliffe Publishing. *Diversity in Health and Social Care 1*, 117–25.

Aronson Fontes, L. (2005) *Child Abuse and Culture: Working with Diverse Families*. New York, NY: Guilford Press.

Atkinson, D., Morten, G. and Sue, D.W. (1989) *Counselling American Minorities: A Cross-Cultural Perspective*. Dubuque, IA: William C. Brown.

Audit Commission (2004) *The Journey to Race Equality*. London: Audit Commission.

Bridges, W. (1991) *Managing Transitions: Making the Most of Change*. Cambridge, MA: Perseus Books.

Buchanan, D. and Huczynski, A. (1991) *Organizational Behaviour: An Introductory Text*. London: Prentice Hall.

Byron, T. (2008) *Safer Children in a Digital World: The Report of the Byron Review*. Nottingham: Department for Children, Schools and Families. Also available at: www.education.gov. uk/publications

Bywaters, P. and Harris, A. (1998) 'Supporting carers: Is practice still sexist?' *Health and Social Care in the Community 6*, 6, 458–63.

Carter, R.T. (1990) 'Does race or racial identity attitudes influence the counselling process in Black/White dyads?' In J.E. Helms (ed.) *Black and White Racial Identity Attitudes: Theory, Research, and Practice*, (pp. 145–164). Westport, CT: Greenwood Press.

Christian Legal Centre, The (2011) 'High Court Judgment suggests Christian beliefs harmful to children. Fostering by Christians now in doubt.' Available at www. christianconcern.com/christian-legal-centre.

Community Care Live (2008) *'CCLive: Social workers have "conservative" attitudes on sexuality'* by Maria Ahmed. Available at www.communitycare.co.uk.

Conroy Grizzle Associates (2001) *Recruiting, Retaining and Progressing the Careers of Minority Ethnic Staff in the Probation Service*. London: Home Office Publications.

Court, D. and Durrance, P. (2008) *The Greenwich and Lewisham Hate Crime Project*. London: Probation Service.

Cross, S.B., Kaye, E. and Ratnofsky, A.C. (1993) *A Report on the Maltreatment of Children with Disabilities*. Washington, DC: National Center on Child Abuse and Neglect.

Dale, E. (1969) *Audio-visual Methods in Teaching*. New York, NY: Holt, Rinehart and Winston.

Department for Children, Schools and Families (2009) *Safeguarding Disabled Children: Practice Guidance*. London: DCSF.

Department for Education (2011) *Adoption: National Minimum Standards*. London: DfE.

Department for Education and Skills (2007) *Safeguarding Children from Abuse Linked to a Belief in Spirit Possession*. London: DfES Publications.

Department of Health (2010) *A Vision for Adult Social Care: Capable Communities and Active Citizens.* London: DoH.

Department of Health, Department for Education and Employment, and Home Office (2000) *Framework for the Assessment of Children in Need and their Families.* London: DfH.

Department of Health and Department for Education and Skills (2007) *Good Practice Guidance on Working with Parents with a Learning Disability.* London: DoH/DfES.

Dick, S. (2008) 'Homophobic Hate Crime: The Gay British Crime Survey.' Stonewall. Available at www.stonewall.org.uk

Doel, M. and Shardlow, M. (2005) *Modern Social Work Practice: Teaching and Learning in Practice Settings.* Aldershot: Ashgate Publishing.

Drake, R. (1996) 'A critique of the role of the traditional charities.' In L. Barton (ed.) *Disability and Society: Emerging Issues and Insight.* Essex: Addison Wesley Longman.

Dreyfus, H.L. and Dreyfus, S.E. (1986) *Mind over Machine: The Power of Human Intuition and Expertise in the Era of the Computer.* Oxford: Basil Blackwell.

Durkin, K. and Barber, B. (2002) 'Not so doomed: Computer game play and positive adolescent development.' *Journal of Applied Developmental Psychology 23,* 373–92.

Emerson, E., Malam, S., Davides, I. and Spencer, K. (2005) *Adults with Learning Difficulties in England 2003/4.* London: NHS Health and Social Care Information Centre.

French, J.R.P. and Raven, B. (1959) *Studies in Social Power.* Ann Arbor, MI: University of Michigan.

Gast, L. (2000) Unpublished. Research done as part of training courses.

General Social Care Council (2010) *Code of Practice for Social Care Workers and Code of Practice for Employers of Social Care Workers.* London: GSCC.

Goleman, D. (1996) *Emotional Intelligence.* London: Bloomsbury.

Goswami, U. (2008) *Child Development: Research Review for the Byron Review on the Impact of New Technologies on Children.* London: Department for Children, Families and Schools.

Gross, T. (2008) 'Recognition of immaturity and emotional expressions in blended faces by children with autism and other developmental disorders.' *Journal of Autism and Developmental Disorders 38,* 2, 297–311.

Guirdham, M. (2002) *Interactive Behaviour at Work.* Basingstoke: Prentice Hall.

Guirdham, M. (2005) *Communicating across Cultures at Work,* 2nd edition. West Lafayette, IN: Ichor Books.

Harrison, R., Harvey, R. and Maclean, S. (2010) *Developing Cultural Competence in Social and Health Care.* Staffordshire: Kirwin Maclean Associates.

Haslam, S.A., Oakes, P. J., McGarty, C., Turner, J.C., Reynolds, K.J. and Eggins, R.A. (1996) 'Stereotyping and social influence: Mediation of stereotype applicability and sharedness by the views of ingroups and outgroup members.' *British Journal of Social Psychology 35,* 3, 369–97.

Higgins, M. and Swain, J. (2010) *Disability and Child Sexual Abuse Lessons from Survivors' Narratives for Effective Protection, Prevention and Treatment.* London: Jessica Kingsley Publishers.

HM Inspectorate of Probation (2000) *Thematic Inspection Report: Towards Race Equality.* London: Home Office.

Hofstede, G. (1984) *Culture's Consequences: International Differences in Work-Related Values.* Thousand Oaks, CA: Sage.

Hofstede, G. (2001) *Culture's Consequences: Comparing Values, Behaviors, Institutions and Organizations across Nations*, 2nd edn. Thousand Oaks, CA: Sage. Hofstede's own websites: www.geerthofstede.nl/geert.aspx; www.geert-hofstede.com/hofstede_dimensions.php – for a summary of the positions of different countries on the four dimensions.

Honey, P. and Mumford, A. (1982) *Manual of Learning Styles*. Coventry: Peter Honey Publishing.

Honey, P. and Mumford, A. (1983) *Using Your Learning Styles*. Maidenhead: Peter Honey Publications.

Honey, P. and Mumford, A. (2006) *The Learning Styles Questionnaire: 80-item Version*. Maidenhead: Peter Honey Publications.

International Federation of Social Workers (IFSW) (2000) 'Definition of Social Work'. www.ifsw.org/

International Federation of Social Workers (IFSW) (2004) *Ethics in Social Work, Statement of Principles*. Available at www.ifsw.org

Jung, C.G. (1971, first published 1921) *Psychological Types*. London: Routledge.

Kennedy, M. (1989) 'The abuse of deaf children.' *Child Abuse Review 3*, 1.

Keirsey, D. and Bates, M. (1978) *Please Understand Me: Character and Temperament Types*. San Diego, CA: Prometheus Nemesis.

Keirsey, D. and Bates, M. (1998) *Please Understand Me II: Temperament, Character, Intelligence*. San Diego, CA: Prometheus Nemesis.

Kluckhohn, C. and Murray, H.A. (eds) (1948) *Personality in Nature, Society and Culture*. New York, NY: Knopf.

Kolb, D.A. (1984) *Experiential Learning: Experiences as the Source of Learning Development*. Upper Saddle River, NJ: Prentice Hall.

Kübler-Ross, E. (1969) *On Death and Dying*. New York, NY: Macmillan.

Lakoff, R.T. (1975) *Language and Woman's Place*. New York: Octagon Books.

Lakoff, R. (2004) *Language and Woman's Place*. New York, NY: Oxford University Press.

Laming, H. (2003) *The Victoria Climbié Inquiry Report*. London: HMSO.

Maslow, A.H. (1954) *Motivation and Personality*. New York, NY: Harper & Row.

McGuire, J. (2000) *Cognitive Behavioural Approaches: An Introduction to Theory and Research*. London: Home Office and HMIP.

McPherson, W. (2001) *Enquiry into the Death of Stephen Lawrence*. London: HMSO.

Mencap (2007) *Bullying Wrecks Lives: The Experiences of Children and Young People with a Learning Disability*. London: Mencap.

Morris, J. (1991) *Pride Against Prejudice*. London: The Women's Press.

Morrison, T. (2001) *Staff Supervision in Social Care*. Brighton: Pavilion.

Morrison, T. (2010) 'The strategic leadership of complex practice.' *Child Abuse Review 27*, 2, 312–29.

Morrison, T. (2010) *NQSW & EPD Guide for Supervisors*. Leeds: Children's Welfare Development Council (CWDC).

Munro, E. (2008) *Effective Child Protection*. London: Sage.

Munro, E. (2010) *The Munro Review Part One: A Systems Analysis*. London: Department for Education.

Munro, E. (2011a) *The Munro Review of Child Protection Interim Report: The Child's Journey.* London: Department for Education.

Munro, E. (2011b) *The Munro Review of Child Protection: Final Report: A Child-Centred System.* London: Department for Education.

Myers, I. and Briggs, K. (1987) *Introduction to Type: A Description of the Theory and Applications of the Myers/Briggs Type Indicator.* Palo Alto, CA: Consulting Psychologists Press.

Namaganda, S. (2004) *Information for People with Learning Disabilities from Black and Minority Ethnic Groups.* Bristol: Norah Fry Research Centre.

Parrott, B., MacIver, A. and Thoburn, J. (2007) *Independent Inquiry Report into the Circumstances of Child Sexual Abuse by Two Foster Carers in Wakefield.* Wakefield District Safeguarding Children Board.

Pilkington, A. (2003) *Racial Disadvantage and Ethnic Diversity in Britain.* Basingstoke: Palgrave Macmillan.

Quarmby, K. (2008) *Getting Away with Murder: Disabled People's Experiences of Hate Crime in the UK.* London: Scope.

Qureshi, H. and Walker, A. (1989) *The Caring Relationship. Elderly People and their Families.* Basingstoke: Macmillan.

Reder, P., Duncan, S. and Gray, M. (1993) *Beyond Blame: Child Abuse Tragedies Revisited.* London: Routledge.

Robinson, C. and Stalker, K. (eds) (1998) *Growing up with Disability.* London: Jessica Kingsley Publishers.

Rueda, M.R., Rothbart, M.K., McCandliss, B.D., Saccomanno, L. and Posner, M.I. (2005) 'Training, maturation, and genetic influences on the development of executive attention.' *Proceedings of the National Academy of Sciences of the United States of America 102,* 41, 14931–6.

Senge P. (1990) *The Fifth Discipline.* New York, NY: Doubleday.

Sin, C.H., Hedges, A., Cook, C., Mguni, N. and Comber, N. (2009) *Disabled People's Experiences of Targeted Violence and Hostility.* Manchester: Equality and Human Rights Commission. Research Report 21.

Sobsey, D. (1994) *Violence and Abuse in the Lives of People with Disability: The End of Silent Acceptance?* Baltimore, MD: Paul Brookes Publishing.

Social Work Reform Board (SWRB) (2010) *Social Work Reform Board – One Year On Report.* London: Department for Education.

Staniland, L. (2009) *Public Perceptions of Disabled People Evidence from the British Social Attitudes Survey 2009.* London: Office for Disability Issues (HM Government).

Stonewall (1996) *Queer Bashing.* London: Stonewall. www.stonewall.org.uk

Stonewall (2009) *Hate Crimes and Hate Incidents.* Produced by Stonewall for the Equalities and Human Rights Commission – available in digital format only at www.stonewall.org.uk.

Sullivan, P.M. and Knutson, J.F. (1997) *Maltreatment and Disabilities: A School Based Epidemiological Study.* Omaha, NE: St Joseph's Service League Center for Abused Handicapped Children.

Tannen, D. (1989) *That's Not What I Meant.* London: Virago.

Tannen, D. (1995) *Talking From 9 to 5: Women and Men at Work.* London: Virago.

Tannen, D. (2001) *You Just Don't Understand: Men and Women in Conversation.* London: Virago.

Taylor, P. and Gast, L. (2003) *Responsivity in Practice: Ideas for Engaging with and Motivating Learners.* Malvern: Linda and Mike Gast Training. Available at training@lindagast.co.uk

Thompson, N. (1998) *Promoting Equality: Challenging Discrimination and Oppression in the Human Services.* Basingstoke: Macmillan.

Thompson, N. *Anti-discriminatory Practice* (4th edn) (2001) Basingstoke: Palgrave Macmillan.

Thompson, N. (2006) *Anti-Discriminatory Practice,* 4th edition. Basingstoke: Palgrave Macmillan.

Thompson, N. (2011) *Promoting Equality: Working with Diversity and Difference.* Basingstoke: Palgrave Macmillan.

Training Organisation for the Personal Social Services (TOPSS) (2002) *The UK National Occupation Standards for Social Work.* Leeds: (TOPSS).

Ulph, F., Betts, P., Mulligan, J. and Stratford, R.J. (2004) *Personality Functioning: The Influence of Stature.* Southampton: University of Southampton.

Watson, A.K., Munroe, E.E. and Atterstrom, H. (1989) 'Comparison of communication apprehension across cultures: American and Swedish children.' *Communication Quarterly* 37, 1.

Westcott, H. and Cross, M. (1996) *This Far and No Further: Towards Ending the Abuse of Disabled Children.* Birmingham: Venture Press.

Whitley, B.E. and Kite, M.E. (2010) *The Psychology of Prejudice and Discrimination.* Belmont, CA: Wadsworth.

Wiffin, J. (2010) *Family Perspectives on Safeguarding and on Relationships with Children's Services.* London: Office of the Children's Commissioner. Available at www.childrenscommissioner.gov.uk

Wonnacott, J. (2012) *Mastering Social Work Supervision.* London: Jessica Kingsley Publishers.

Wonnacott, J. and Kennedy, M. (2001) 'A model approach.' *Community Care* 8–14 March.

SUBJECT INDEX

AUTHOR INDEX